D0369227

Picking up the Threads
The Colours of World Football

John Chandler

Pitch Publishing Ltd
A2 Yeoman Gate
Yeoman Way
Durrington
BN13 3QZ

Email: info@pitchpublishing.co.uk
Web: www.pitchpublishing.co.uk

First published by Pitch Publishing 2012

A CIP catalogue record for this book is available from the British Library.

13-digit ISBN: 9781908051363
Design and page layout by Brilliant Orange Sports Management.
Printed in Malta. Manufacturing managed by Jellyfish Print Solutions Ltd.

Picking up the Threads
The Colours of World Football

John Chandler

To Graceland FC
and all those who have chipped in,
especially Sarah.

Contents

Introduction

The Boca jersey is more than just a simple piece of sporting attire.

It is the treasure of each fan who asks that their players sweat for them until their last drop.

It is the sacred cloak for which hundreds of songs have been created in its honour.

It is the symbol that unites all the xeneizes* scattered around the world.

It is the blood, soul, and heart of a fan with unconditional love for Boca.

It is that which has been shown off by idols for more than a century of fervour and passion; **it is the jersey of Boca.**

Mantra of Argentina's Boca Juniors

The words of Boca Juniors sum up the feeling fans worldwide have for their team's colours; the phrase 'not fit to wear the shirt' can be heard on any radio phone-in after yet another lacklustre display. These colours, which are as ingrained into supporters as our team's anthems and achievements, were often chosen over a century ago. The stories of how the world's teams came to wear their colours are as fascinating and diverse as the teams and cultures they come from.

In 1993 a group of friends who worked at the Lakeside branch of Tesco decided that there was more to life than groceries and set about forming a Sunday League team. A name was decided on, Delamare FC, after the street in which Tesco's head office is situated; and then the problem of a kit, what colour should it be; Tesco's corporate colours are red, white and blue? Most of the team were West Ham fans so claret and blue? The majority lived in the town of Grays, so grey? Practicalities won out over these more metaphoric reasons and on the principal "beggars can't be choosers" and someone at Tesco having a spare kit, Delamare FC ran out in the Circus Tavern Sunday League Division Four in a black and white striped kit. The away kit was a horrifying set of yellow shirts with holes in, donated by a wealthier team who could afford to replace theirs on a regular basis. There were only ten of these away shirts, so subs had to come on and swap with the mud- and sweat-ridden player coming off. Parting company with Tesco after the UK's biggest retailer refused to get the team another kit and consequently changing their name to Graceland FC (one too many Elvis fans in the club), the team soldiered on for a couple more years with kits coming from bankrupt stock, but soon Graceland FC had enough money to choose their colours. This next strip was a far cry from the first away kit, in the style of Ajax of Amsterdam, but with a deep blue panel, the sides a blood red, a strip to be proud of. What was the reason behind

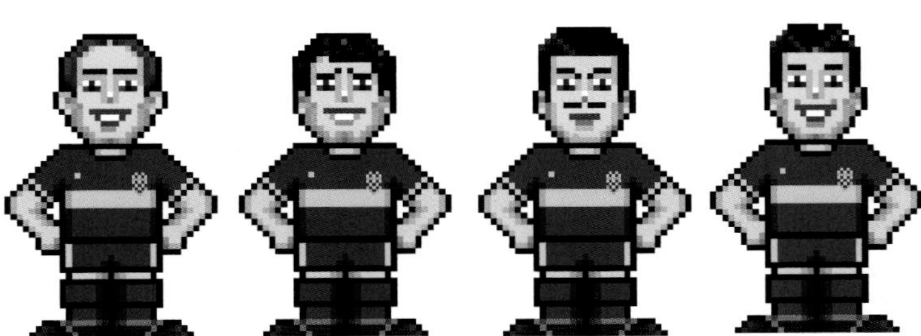

this glorious combination of colours? Somewhat romantically for a team from South Essex, the colours were chosen by the manager, Yorky, as his European team was Barcelona and he wanted to get a kit with their colours. Why was Barcelona his European team? An ex-girlfriend of his came from Barcelona and he used to go to the games with her, whilst visiting the Catalan city. With the hope that one Sunday, he would be able to stand on the sidelines and sing "It's just like watching Barça!" Sadly that day never dawned, with Graceland FC never quite getting any higher than Division Two of the Circus Tavern League.

The thing is; one hundred years or so ago, when football was in its infancy, the argument between amateurism and professionalism still raging, the FA Cup still contested at cricket's Kensington Oval ground, Graceland's story would not have been that dissimilar to teams that would one day become Manchester United or Chelsea. In fact, as Graceland started out as a Tesco works team, so did Manchester United start out as Newton Heath LYR, a team representing the Lancashire & Yorkshire Railway and West Ham United was formed from Thames Ironworks, a shipbuilders' firm team. This phenomenon was not just an English one. The French club A.S. Saint-Étienne was formed by workers from the French grocery chain Casino. So how did these teams end up wearing the colours that they are famous for today? Was it because their manager managed to secure a strip off a rival at an economically challenging time and the colours stuck, evolving over time to being the traditional colours tied to FA Cups? Or is there a more romantic reason that the colours became associated with a team and ended up being waved on scarves in the stands of Anfield and the Bernabeu?

In this book we will find reasons behind the colours of some of the most famous clubs in the world that stretch back to their foundation and are every bit as romantic as an ex-girlfriend's love of Barcelona.

* The fans of Boca Juniors are known as los xeneizes (the Genoese) after the Genoese immigrants who founded the team.

You lot can go skins
A brief history of how to tell who's who

The evolution of the game of Association Football is a long and twisting tale that would need much more than a brief introduction to do justice to, but its early history has gone some way to influence the colours of many of today's teams and bears looking into in those terms. Football, as we know it today, began its transition from massive 300-plus-a-side village contests with games such as the famous Eton Wall Game at the public schools of England and was honed and bullied into shape by the first amateur teams of the public schools of Harrow and Eton and the professional teams of Northern England and Scotland in the late 19th century. As today, early gatherings necessitated the use of some way of differentiating teams, but this was by no means an overnight transition to the first, second and sometimes third kits we see today. Many early teams would make use of a single coloured item of clothing, a red cap in the case of Nottingham Forest, a sash similar to those worn by beauty pageant winners or even a white tie as worn by Vasco da Gama of Brazil.

As the game progressed in these early days teams began to play in more complete uniforms. The game and its niceties were still very different from today; the first FA Cup Final in 1872 between Wanderers and Royal Engineers was watched by a crowd of 2,000, while the then rules of football meant that throw-ins were like rugby line-outs, taken one-handed with the ball being thrown onto the pitch only at right angles and ends being changed after every goal. The kits too were largely unrecognisable; players could be seen wearing gaudy shirts, knickerbockers and in the case of the Engineers a cap that looked more like 'Wee-Willy-Winkie's' night cap.

The game continued apace, the Wanderers and Royal Engineers gave way to the professionals of Notts County and Preston North End, the influence of the public schools such as Oxford and Cambridge began to be replaced as they shied away from professionalism and they encouraged the students towards the alternative (and still amateur) code of rugby. The kits developed to ones more recognisable to modern viewers; caps, and knickerbockers becoming things of the past. Still odd things could happen, the struggle between amateurism and professionalism (or the gentlemen and players) led in 1886 to the first acknowledged professional to play for England, J.H. Forrest of Blackburn Rovers, having to wear a different colour shirt from his amateur colleagues in the game against Scotland.

The first FA Cup Final of 1872:
Wanderers vs. Royal Engineers played at the Kennington Oval.
Wanderers won 1-0.

Finer tinkering was to come. In 1890 the Football League stipulated that no two teams could have the same colours, so as to avoid clashes. This rule was only briefly enforced and soon it was ruled that teams must have a second set of shirts available in a different colour. The home team initially was required to change colours in the event of a clash, but by the early 1920s the rule was amended; from now on the away team were to change. In 1909, some 32 years after the first FA Cup Final, a rule was brought in that the goalkeeper had to wear a different coloured shirt to the rest of the team and it wasn't until 1939 that the FA made the numbering of shirts a requirement.

It could have gone other ways too; at the same time across the Atlantic in America, as baseball became their national sport, a novel solution was found to the problem of team differentiation: it was decided that home 'uniforms' for all clubs would be white, while 'road' (away) uniforms were either grey or a darker colour. This solution spread to other US sports, with the 'White home' shirt convention in basketball and college hockey and 'White away' for American football and professional hockey. Further details have been added over the years; in baseball, the 'White home' has the added graphics of the team nickname, for example, Boston's home shirt has Red Sox on it, and when 'on the road' they have their city name on it. Special one-off jerseys for significant holidays appear. Taking Boston as an example

The Originals, the founder members of the Football League in their 1889 colours.

again, who, with their strong Irish connections, wear a green shirt for St. Patrick's Day games.

Meanwhile, football was soon spreading beyond the shores of Britain, taken by Scottish and English engineers, mineral miners and sailors to all corners of the Empire and South America and Europe. In a similar way to English and Scottish clubs these teams would find their colours over the years for varying reasons. In some cases the colours would come from the Anglo importers of the game, while in the Netherlands the Dutch briefly brought in a rule similar to the FA's one team-one colour rule. In many European and South American cities, football teams sprung up attached to the various sports clubs. These clubs brought everything from rowing to basketball under one roof, and often the colours would carry over all these sports.

Though most club sides went through at least one change of colours

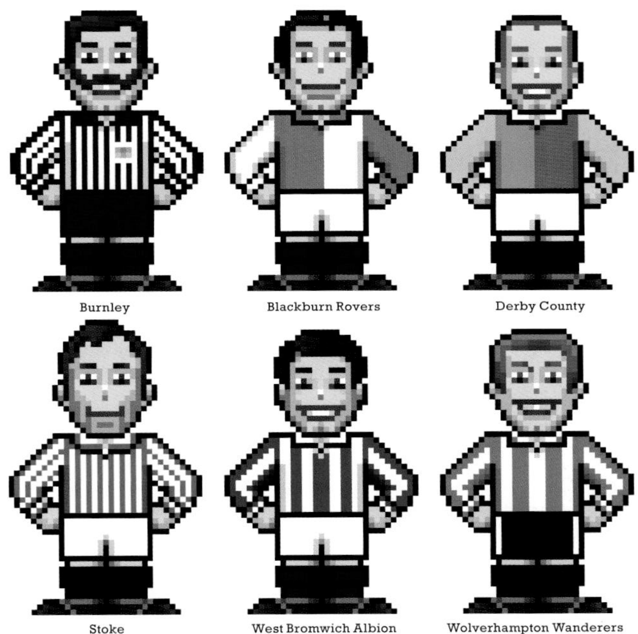

Burnley · Blackburn Rovers · Derby County

Stoke · West Bromwich Albion · Wolverhampton Wanderers

in their early years, slowly and steadily teams worldwide stopped tinkering with their colours; a kit from most English and Scottish league teams' 1920 season would be almost indistinguishable from a 1970s' kit.

International teams too became more popular, the World Cup coming into being in 1930. Colours representing the nation's pride soon became set in stone, though this could still sometimes cause bizarre events, such as the third-place play-off at the Italian World Cup of 1934. The fierce rivals Austria and Germany both wore the same first kit (white shirts, black shorts). Both teams refused to change and it wasn't until Germany scored and many spectators presumed Austria had gone ahead, that the referee stopped the game and insisted Germany change into a different shirt, which, for the records, was red.

Today's modern game is thankfully largely free of such mix-ups, however as football has become a worldwide multi-billion pound industry the humble football kit has moved a further stage from the red cap of Nottingham Forest. Jeremy Leslie and Patrick Burgoyne argue in their book *FC Football Graphics* that often the most distinguishing characteristics of a [modern] team's on-field identity is its sponsor's name. Certainly since the 1980s sponsors' logos and other changes have become the norm; sponsors' logos on the front and sometimes back of shirts and league logos. Strips that haven't changed for years suddenly changing yearly to maximise a club's income; thinner stripes, thicker stripes, a slight change to a collar, chevrons, shadow stripes, badges and symbols interwoven into the fabric. This led to some unpopular kits, for example, who can forget for all the wrong reasons the infamous grey England away kit, which replaced the more traditional red for the Euro 96 campaign, much to the chagrin of the fans? Arsenal's 'chevron' shirt of 91-93? Hull City's tiger stripe design of 1992? Or possibly most infamous of all the 1996 grey Manchester Utd kit, designed to go with jeans, but hated by the players so much that it was changed at half-time in a defeat to Southampton as the players complained they couldn't see each other against the crowd?

In 1996 the latest attempt to introduce football to the USA meant that ten franchises were granted to the newly formed MLS sides. Unlike the somewhat organic growth of the European and South American teams of the 19th century, the new teams were started from scratch. Marketing officials, from the league, from Nike and from Adidas came together to construct the teams and their colours. Sometimes the marketing and commercialism scream out, guess the colours of the New York Red Bulls anyone?

So where next? As an almost inevitable backlash to the 1980s and 90s, the excesses of kit design at least in the UK seem to be calming down with the outlandish becoming less fashionable. Undoubtedly the seasonal changes are here to stay, the financial situation in football not allowing such a lucrative revenue stream to dry up. Styles will continue to change, the only saving grace has been that, with a handful of exceptions (such as those mentioned above) the traditional colours have remained the same. It seems most clubs and countries are aware that some things are sacrosanct, a hundred years of history is impossible to just dismiss even though some marketing men may want to. So let's hope that for the next hundred years we fans can continue to, on behalf of our clubs, bleed red, or, blue, or claret, or black and white, or...

picking up the threads

English and Welsh Club Teams

ACCRINGTON STANLEY

There have been three major clubs in Accrington and all have worn red kits. The first club, who were just called Accrington were founder members of the Football League folding, in 1896. The first Accrington Stanley were formed in 1891 folding in 1966, and a new team unconnected with the original Stanley were formed in 1968. The reason for the choice of red is unknown, could it be in connection to Lancashire's red rose? Or maybe the town coat-of-arms which is also largely red? Either unfortunately is pure conjecture.

ALDERSHOT TOWN

The team from the Hampshire garrison town was formed after the original Aldershot FC was wound up in 1992. The newly formed Aldershot Town took the colours of the old club; which in turn came as a reflection of the town's close association with the Army and thus the Union Jack. As with many teams that have had a rocky history, Aldershot have had many styles of shirt from plain red shirts to stripes and even a quartered style in 2006.

ARSENAL

The development of Arsenal's famous kit came in two stages. When still called Dial Square in 1895, two years before the club became professional, a small group of Nottingham Forest players, Charlie Bates, Fred Beardsley and Bill Parr were signed and brought their old kits of plain red along with them. Not having the financial clout of today, the club decided the cheapest way of acquiring a complete strip was to kit the team out in the same colour as the ex-Forest players. Beardsley, it is thought, wrote to his old club who provided a set of the Nottingham club's dark 'Garibaldi Red' shirts (see p40).

Herbert Chapman the innovative manager (who also pioneered the influential 'WM' formation and had the famous clock installed at Highbury) instigated the next stage of the Arsenal kit's development. Chapman, depending on what source is to be believed, either noticed a groundsman wearing a red sleeveless sweater over a white shirt or played golf with the famous cartoonist of the time, Tom Webster, who was wearing something similar.

Either way, the combination inspired the manager to create a new strip which he believed to be more visible for his players combining the (by this time brighter) red shirt with white collar and sleeves.

ASTON VILLA

As one of England's oldest clubs, Aston Villa's early kits went through many changes before they settled on their now famous claret and blue. Strips of green and even an all black shirt with a red lion were worn before a strip described as chocolate and blue seemingly evolved to the claret and blue combination. The style of having contrasting body and sleeves was introduced in the late 19th century, designed by Ollie Whateley, a player who had been a graphic designer before he had joined the club. The distinctive design became

very successful and it was often referred to as the 'Villa style' when used by other clubs, even when the colours were of a different combination. The combination has been taken up by a number of other English clubs, but interestingly is rarely seen outside of England.

BARNET

When the London club merged with Alston Works AFC, a team from a false teeth factory nicknamed

'The Dentals' in 1912, they took on board Alston's amber and black kit, which they have worn in various combinations to this day. They have worn the colours in a striped style as well as hooped and with plain amber and in recent years black shirts too.

BARNSLEY

Barnsley once wore blue and white striped shirts. Upon joining the Football League in 1897, Barnsley's

first home fixture was against Loughborough who, in the days before away kits, arrived to play in their similarly striped kit. As one team clearly needed to change, Barnsley changed into red shirts and promptly won 9-0. Possibly taking this as a lucky omen, the red was adopted as Barnsley's permament colour of choice.

BIRMINGHAM CITY

Though the blue and white of Birmingham City suits the club's home, St Andrew's, and the colours associated with the patron Saint of Scotland and his cross, there is no connection between the Saint and Birmingham's choice of colours. Birmingham in fact took their colours from the team they had evolved from, Small Heath Alliance, when like many small teams they upped their ambitions, changed their name and moved into the new St Andrew's stadium at the start of the 20th century; why Small Heath chose blue and white is unfortunately unknown.

BLACKBURN ROVERS

One of the original teams that made up the Football League, Blackburn Rovers, have worn their halved blue and white shirts since 1882, making it one of the most consistent designs in football history. The only changes have been slight, originally the shirts were of a darker Oxford blue, but became a lighter Cambridge blue probably due to players' connections to the Oxbridge universities. The blue moved from left to right and back again until 1935 when it settled on the left where it has remained ever since.

BLACKPOOL

Blackpool's club director, Albert Hargreaves, was also an international referee. He officiated on the 1923 game between the Netherlands and Belgium. The story goes that Hargreaves loved the Dutch colours and as no one else wore them in England he had his club side change to the new colour. Blackpool, however, do not refer to the colour as orange, as the Dutch national team do, but cite it as 'Tangerine'.

BOLTON WANDERERS

Before adopting their white and blue colour scheme the Wanderers had worn a number of strips including perhaps the strangest ever seen in English football consisting of a white shirt with red

spots said to represent the wounds received by soldiers in the Boer War. Their more recognisable strip, though by no means certain, is thought to have been acquired from fellow Lancashire club Turton FC. Turton were an already established club and it is possible the shirts were either given to Bolton or brought along by players joining the club from Turton. The style changed little over the years until the flourishes of the commercial era came in.

AFC BOURNEMOUTH

The question is: what came first, the nickname or the kit? The 'Cherries' nickname is supposed to be a reference to orchards near Bournemouth's pitch. It is, however, unclear whether the red shirts came from the nickname or the nickname from the colour choice!

What is certain is the change to the AC Milan-style shirts, which have often featured for the club, was instigated by manager and former West Ham player John Bond. Bond had been part of a Hammers side beaten 6-0 in a 1954 friendly by the Italians and associated Milan's display with football at its peak.

(See also Man City p32)

BRADFORD CITY

The Yorkshire team play in an amber and claret strip in homage to the colours of the football club Manningham FC and also the colours of the Prince of Wales's Own (Yorkshire) Regiment. Since the 1985 Valley Parade fire which claimed the lives of 56 people, Bradford City have incorporated black into their kits.

BRENTFORD

Although it is conjecture, Brentford probably chose red and white as their colours in the 1920s as they are the main colours of the Middlesex coat of arms. The coat of arms often appeared as part of the team's badge and an area's crest is not an uncommon source of inspiration for clubs who want to tie themselves to a particular area.

BRIGHTON & HOVE ALBION

Brighton's early shirts have been described as 'Fisherman's blue', a historic navy colour of Scottish origin often associated with the maritime trade and perhaps suited to a seaside town. The colour has changed to a more royal blue over the years and the white stripes have been incorporated for most of the club's history.

There has also been a suggestion that the club had early links with West Bromwich Albion and this may have had links to the colour choice as well, but this could be a red herring.

BRISTOL CITY

The coat of arms of Bristol is largely red and white; whether

this is the reason Bristol City chose this combination and have stuck with it since the 1890s is unknown, but like many other English clubs, Bristol City used the town's crest as a team badge for a time in the days before graphic designers.

BRISTOL ROVERS

In 1931 the then manager of Rovers, Albert Prince-Cox brought in the

blue and white quartered shirt in order to make the players look bigger and more intimidating (a technique often used by rugby clubs). The quarters have not been static with the blue squares often being diagonally opposite to the illustration.

BURNLEY

Green was once considered an unlucky colour; in early English folklore, witches, the devil, faeries and spirits all wore or were green. There is also a saying that if a woman wears a

green gown for a wedding the next gown she wears will be black.

Burnley's original colour was green, but legend has it that an old lady told them the significance of their choice so they changed to the colours of one of the then most successful teams in England, Aston Villa, and they have been in claret and blue ever since.

BURY

Bury were formed from two church teams and though it is speculation, it is thought the white was chosen as their shirt colour as a symbol of purity associated

with the church. The town's coat of arms is also blue and white and has always formed the basis of the club's badge so again, speculating only; this also could have been a deciding factor for the Greater Manchester club choice of white and blue.

CAMBRIDGE UNITED

It may seem surprising that, given that many early English teams took their colours from the Oxbridge universities, Cambridge don't wear light blue. Had Cambridge's history stretched back to football's early days and the influence of the public schools they probably would. However they only came into being in 1951 when Abbey Utd changed their name as part of a drive to

achieve greater things. They had played in various combinations of yellow and black, and these colours carried over to the new team, although why Abbey Utd originally chose them is unfortunately unknown.

CARDIFF CITY

The 'Bluebirds' have played in blue since 1908; however new Malaysian

owners have instigated a controversial rebrand with a new badge and red shirts for the 2012 season.

Red is considered a lucky colour in many Eastern countries, and the move is designed to appeal to this lucrative market.

CHARLTON ATHLETIC

The group of boys who founded Charlton borrowed a set of the then all-red shirts of South London

neighbours Woolwich Arsenal (who would later drop the Woolwich after their move to North London). The colours have remained to this day.

DID YOU SEE THAT TACKLE? THEY'RE BOTH GOING TO BE SO COVERED IN MUD WE'LL HAVE TROUBLE TELLING THEM APART!

YOU'RE RIGHT! THAT'S WHY THE FA BANNED BROWN SHIRTS UNLESS HALVED UNTIL 1992!

CHELSEA

Chelsea were formed in 1905 when builder Gus Mears needed a team to play in his newly redeveloped Stamford Bridge stadium after Fulham refused because the rent was too high! The chosen colours of the new team were the blue and white racing colours of Lord Chelsea the Earl of Cadogan, the first president (see p80). Originally the blue was lighter, the shorts white and socks black. The blue changed, over the years, to a more royal blue colour.

The full evolution of the kit was down to 60s manager Tommy Docherty, who changed the shorts to match the shirt and also altered the socks to white, to make the colour scheme more modern and distinctive.

CHESTER CITY

Though the reason for the introduction of the blue and white stripes of Chester City is unknown it is known at least who was responsible. Charlie Hewitt, the then manager, changed the colours in 1930 from black and white stripes and the colours have stayed largely unchanged since.

CHESTERFIELD

A strong identification with Britishness runs through Chesterfield kits; the Derbyshire team's early shirts were more often than not red, white or blue and they even sported a Union Jack shirt in 1882. Whether this is why, in the main, blue first kits and red away have been their colours is not certain.

COLCHESTER UNITED

When the amateur team Colchester Town folded to essentially allow a new professional team to be set up in the Essex town in 1937, the team that replaced them, Colchester United, took their colours as well as their place. Why Town originally chose blue and white is sadly unknown. United have usually worn the blue and white colours in a striped style, although other combinations have been used, such as all-blue in the early 70s.

COVENTRY CITY

As well as being a famous football pundit, Jimmy Hill was a revolutionary figure in post-war football. He was a leading figure in the abolishment of the maximum wage for footballers and in club management he was also an innovator. Hill introduced the all-sky-blue kit at Coventry in 1961 while manager of the club.

The strip harked back to early turn of the century Coventry kits, while the matching shorts and socks gave it a modern feel in a combination unique to English football. The strip was part of a series of innovations designed to modernise the club nicknamed "The Sky Blue Revolution". Hill and the club's board oversaw redevelopment of the stadium, pre-match entertainment, a re-designed match-day programme as well as even writing the club song "The Sky Blue Song", sung to the tune of the Eton Boating Song.

CRYSTAL PALACE

Through the history of football a change of colours has often been used in an attempt to breathe new life into a club or herald a new beginning. Few clubs have had as many new beginnings as the often troubled South London club. The original colours came courtesy of Aston Villa who donated a kit to the fledgling Crystal Palace and the famous claret and blue combination became the mainstay of their strips until the first new start led to a change to white shirts in the 1940s.

Short term changes continued; first back to the Villa style, then white with a claret and blue band, then all-white in homage to Real Madrid, back to claret and blue, but this time in pin-stripe style and then a combination of the two with a white strip with a thick claret and blue stripe.

Malcolm Allison was made manager in 1973 and as during his time at Manchester City instigated a kit change, the claret and sky-blue changing to bright red and blue stripes. Another new start saw Terry Venables and the return of the Madrid strip now with a red and blue sash. (See p51).

The colours have for the time settled down, the red and blue striped shirt being the combination mostly favoured since the late 1980s.

The away shirt has also had new beginnings; in the 90s it was modelled on Brazil's kit, while the popular white shirt with blue and red sash has appeared again as the away kit in recent years.

DAGENHAM & REDBRIDGE

With the latest in a long line of mergers and takeovers of various Essex and East London clubs leading to the formation of Dagenham and Redbridge Forest in 1992, the red and blue colours of the two teams were combined to form the basis of the new kit for the new club.

DERBY COUNTY

Originally associated with the county cricket club, Derby started their days wearing the chocolate, amber and light blue colours of the cricket club. It is thought the move away from these colours as an attempt to differentiate the team from its parent club.

EVERTON

Everton began their life as St Domino, a church team playing in blue and white stripes, becoming Everton in 1879. The new club faced a problem as in those days, players joining from other teams, often due to the cost of replacing a jersey, would continue to wear the colours of their former club. Wanting a unified kit, Everton solved this problem by dyeing all the various shirts of their players black with a red sash added. This strip led to the early Everton nickname The Black Watch after the famous Highland military regiment. Everton had other colours during their early days (including the pink that has resurfaced recently as an away kit) before settling on the royal blue that has become synonymous with the club since 1901.

EXETER CITY

Like many other clubs from the South West, Exeter started their days playing in green. As was the case with other teams (see Burnley p20) they believed their original colours of green to be unlucky so in 1910 they changed to red and white stripes after a poor start to the season. With the later introduction of black shorts Exeter's colours mirror those seen on the town's coat of arms.

FULHAM

Formed from the church team Fulham St Andrews, the West London club have worn their white shirts since their earliest days. There is no evidence why white was chosen, perhaps similarly to Bury the white comes from its association with the church? (see Bury p21).

In 2010 Fulham wore a change strip of green and gold in homage to the livery of the up-market department store Harrods. Club owner Mohamed al Fayed had a long association with the west end store, being a former owner and the current Chairman.

GILLINGHAM

Formed as New Brompton playing in black and white stripes the club became Gillingham in 1913. In the 1930s the Kent team changed colours and Gillingham played their games in blue. Since the 1990s Gillingham have occasionally worn kits of black and blue, combining the colours of New Brompton with the blue.

HEREFORD UNITED

Hereford's original strip was all-white. The black shorts were added in 1946 when, during the post-war period of a Britain still on rations and experiencing many shortages, the club used material from the now surplus to requirement blackout curtains to make shorts after running out of white material.

HULL CITY

It is not known why Hull decided on a striped kit in the colours of amber and black, but the club soon gained the nickname 'the tigers' because of the distinctive style. The Kingston upon Hull team have often worn plain amber shirts despite the popularity of the striped style and infamously wore a couple of kits in the 1990s that took the tiger motif one stage further with a 'tiger skin' style kit that was unique to say the least!

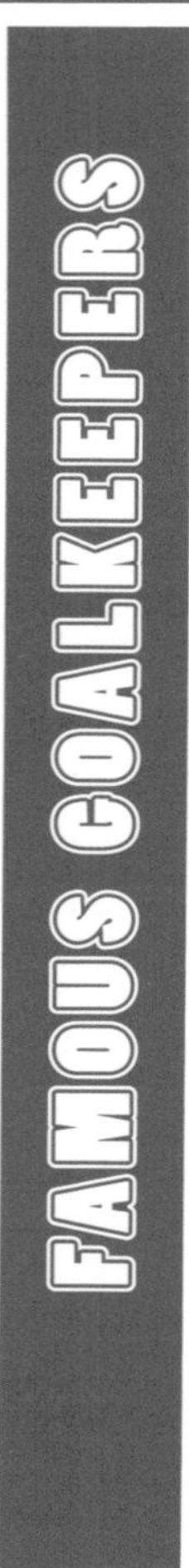

PETER SHILTON England (1949) The most capped England player. Wore the famous England yellow international jersey for most of his caps. 125 ■

DINO ZOFF Italy (1942) Became the oldest player to win the World Cup when Italy won in 1982 wearing his famous grey jersey. Zoff also went on to manage the national team. 112 ■

JORGE CAMPOS Mexico (1966) The popular, eccentric Campos was known for his self-designed multi-coloured kits and was also a gifted striker, scoring 38 club goals. 129 ■

BOB WILSON Arsenal (1941) One of Arsenal's greats. Wore the traditional English club keeper's green between 1963 and 1974 for the Gunners. English by birth, played for Scotland. 2 ■

GORDON BANKS England (1937) Wore blue in the 1970 World Cup against Brazil. His save from a Pelé header is considered by many to be the greatest ever. 73 ■

GILMAR Brazil (1930) Brazil's most successful keeper. Clad in grey, he played in goal for their World Cup winning teams in 1958 and 1962. He also played in the 1966 tournament. 94 ■

PETR ČECH Czech Rep. (1982) Chelsea's Czech goalkeeper is well known for his protective headgear, but his shirt colours are chosen to make him look bigger. 74 ■

LEV YASHIN USSR (1929) Keeper for Dynamo Moscow's football and ice hockey teams. Nicknamed "The Black Spider" because of his talent and kit, was voted the FIFA Goalkeeper of the 20th C. 78 ■

IPSWICH TOWN

Ipswich's first president in 1878 was Conservative MP Thomas Cobbold. It may seem simple to guess that the blue of Ipswich's colour comes from the Tory MP's association with the Party, whose colour is blue, but it may be more complicated than that. The Tories only formalised blue as their official colour in the 1960s, primarily because the rise of the Labour Party and other politically left leaning world parties had made red a 'Socialist' colour. Before then individual MPs would choose their colour; for the majority of Conservative constituencies this was blue, but also red (with its association with the Union Jack) and even gold and green were used. So as to whether Cobbold was a 'true blue' Tory or not is open to conjecture, what is sure is Ipswich have always been 'true blue'.

LEEDS UNITED

The Yorkshire club originally played in the gold and blue of the

borough of Leeds, and changed their colours to all-white in 1961 at the behest of legendary manger Don Revie who had ambitions to transform the clubs fortunes. His idea was to try to emulate the all-conquering Real Madrid (see p51). The gold and blue is now used as trim on the home strip and often for the away strip.

LEICESTER CITY

Formed as Leicester Fosse by old boys from the Wyggeston school,

it is interesting to note that they didn't take the school colours of black, gold and white, playing in blue well before they changed their name to Leicester City in 1919. Why blue? No definitive reason is known, but perhaps the blue was chosen for water, as a fosse is a fortified ditch or canal.

LEYTON ORIENT

The Orient in the East London club's name comes from close links between the club and the Orient Shipping Line (later to become P&O). Known at various times as Clapton Orient and just

plain Orient, for most of their history Leyton Orient has worn the red kit they wear today, but only just! They have also worn a mainly white kit and also a blue kit from 1946 until well into the 60s. There is no record of why the team chose or changed these colours; P&O's corporate colours (red, blue, yellow and white) formed an early team badge, while the predominant colour of the Orient line was yellow, the only colour associated with P&O not to feature majorly for Orient!

LINCOLN CITY

When the local team Lincoln Rovers folded in 1884, Lincoln City emerged from the ashes with many of the Rovers players going over to the new team. Unsurprisingly the new team played in Rovers' red and white stripes as many of the players simply brought their jerseys with them. Since those early days Lincoln City have played in red and white (apart from one early season when 'Lincoln Green' was worn) in various combinations, though most often in the striped design.

LIVERPOOL

Probably to the chagrin of many Everton supporters Liverpool only came into existence because of the blue half of Merseyside. Everton FC were the original tenants of Anfield. The owner, John Houlding, was a brewer and wanted only his beers to be sold inside the ground. Arguments over this issue, a proposed land deal, mistrust between the Tory Houlding and Liberal Everton board and on the amount of rent led Everton to quit Anfield for Goodison Park in 1892. Left with the prospect of an empty stadium Houlding founded Liverpool FC. Incredible as it may seem to today's diehard fans of both clubs, Liverpool began their days playing in a set of blue and white shirts that Everton left behind, with Everton in retaliation changing to dark ruby red. This would have continued and perhaps today's red and blue halves could be reversed for Merseyside derbies, but a few years later Everton returned to their

favoured blue, so Liverpool, further cementing their links with the city, took on the municipal colours of red and white.

Liverpool played out the next sixty years wearing the red shirts, but with white shorts and socks. The all-red strip wasn't introduced until the mid-60s when then manager Bill Shankly brought in the strip as he felt it had a greater impact making the players look '7 foot tall'. This was brought in at first for European games and for cup games, later becoming the regular colour choice in the league. Maybe somewhat gallingly for Liverpool fans, there is also some evidence that this may have been influenced by the club's other main rivals, as Manchester United had worn an all-red kit on occasion in European games.

LUTON TOWN

In the 1920s Luton Town changed from a blue strip to all-white shirts after a league ruling stipulating all clubs should own a set of white shirts to avoid clashes. Rather than have to buy a special set, Luton used these white shirts as their home choice. In the 1970s orange and blue was introduced in an effort to re-invent the club. This coincided with Luton's best spell. A recent 30 point penalty for financial irregularities and relegation from the Football League, has led to the reinstatement of the orange and blue scheme after supporters were asked their opinions on the club colours as they recover.

MACCLESFIELD TOWN

After getting into financial trouble, Macclesfield were re-formed at the end of the Second World War. The kit of blue and white was donated by supporters who gave, in a Britain still on rations, their clothing coupons to the club to purchase the new strip.

MANCHESTER CITY

Manchester City took the Cambridge blue as their colour on their formation in 1894 probably because some players or staff at the time had connections to the university.

The AC Milan-style shirts, that City wore as an away strip

most famously for the 1969 cup final victory over Leicester City and on numerous occasions since, was instigated by then assistant manager and former West Ham player Malcolm Allison. Allison, like John Bond (see Bournemouth p19) had been part of a West Ham team beaten 6-0 in a 1954 floodlit friendly by the Italians and associated Milan's performance that night with football at its very best.

MANCHESTER UNITED

Before becoming one of the world's biggest and most successful clubs, Manchester United were the works team of the Leeds & Yorkshire Railway going under the name of Newton Heath LYR. Newton Heath played in the green and gold of the company, but by 1902 the team were facing financial ruin. The story goes that a St Bernard dog owned by the team's captain Harry Stafford got lost at a club fundraiser and was found by local brewer John Davies who agreed to invest in the team after returning it and learning of the team's situation. Though this story may be apocryphal, Davies did join the board and instigated ambitious changes including the name change that tied the club to the city, a technique used by many other clubs in order to garner wider support. The club badge also changed to the red rose of Lancashire (at this stage much of the city of Manchester came under Lancashire). This probably explains why the club changed its colours to red, white and black to further tie them to the area, though their is no direct evidence of this.

The club used Newton Heath's green and yellow halved shirts in the 1990s as an away kit and the colours have since been adopted by the Manchester United Supporters Trust as a symbol of discontent against the current owner Malcolm Glazer.

MELCHESTER ROVERS

The strip of Roy Race was originally modelled on the successful 1950s Arsenal team. Though the style of the kit was the same as the North London club the colours were chosen by writer Frank S. Pepper and artist Jo Colquhoun as they did not match up to any British club and thus would not alienate any supporters. Over the years, paralleling real life, the kit went through subtle changes;

the blue shorts were dropped and a strip of red and yellow stripes became the iconic kit that the owner of 'Racey's rocket' could be seen wearing in various publications. The kit to the right was the last one that was worn by the Rovers in 2001 before the strip ended.

MIDDLESBROUGH

'Boro's colours have been red and white since 1899. In 1973 manager Jack Charlton introduced the broad white band which often features across the chest on 'Boro kits. Charlton had wanted to change the home shirt to white like the team he had played his club football for, Leeds United, and the band

was seemingly a compromise. The style is popular with fans and is often brought in when the club has designed kits with supporter consultation.

MILLWALL

The club that became Millwall, Millwall Rovers was formed by the

Scottish workers of Morton's Jam factory on the Isle of Dogs. With the majority of the workers being of Scottish extraction the colours of Scotland were chosen and Millwall turn out in a blue and white strip to this day.

MK DONS

After the controversial move that took Wimbledon from its South London roots to Buckinghamshire's Milton Keynes, the new club broke all links with its predecessor and announced the new club colours as white, red and black, the original

colours of Milton Keynes council. Chairman Pete Winkelmen also stated, according to John Brockwell of the MK Dons Supporters' Association, that 'White was chosen as the

home kit as he wanted the club to play football like Inter Milan.' Though you're probably thinking white, red and black are colours more associated with AC Milan rather than their city rivals, a little digging and you'll see that MK Dons' holding company is called Inter MK. Perhaps this shows that the decision to move Wimbledon sixty miles away from their home wasn't the only dubious one taken by the club owners?

MORECAMBE

The assumption is that the club from the Lancashire seaside town chose red, on their inception in 1920, as their shirt's colour because their older local rivals Lancaster City (formerly Town) played in the natural footballing opposite of blue shirts. While of

course the red, white and black that Morecambe run out in are also the colours of the Lancaster Rose.

NEWCASTLE UNITED

Newcastle Utd was formed when the two main clubs of the city, West End and Newcastle East End, merged. The first kit of the club was East End's red and white. In 1894 the club first used the black and white striped shirts, which the reserve team wore. These colours were apparently chosen

for the first team as they weren't associated with either of the teams that had merged to form the new club.

NORTHAMPTON TOWN

Northampton Town is another British team who adopted the municipal colours as their club colours, playing in the claret and white colour scheme since 1899. Although the dark red plain shirts have been the favoured style they have worn it in many other combinations, with such flourishes

as white bands or sleeves. For much of the 70s and 80s white was the predominant colour, with the dark red providing the detail.

PICKING UP THE THREADS
15p
Pride of
PLACE
Including:
Aberdeen, AS Monaco, AS Roma, Bayern Munich, Bradford City, Kyoto Sanga, Northampton Town, Real Valladolid and Wolverhampton Wanderers.

Location, location, location.

Most teams are inextricably linked with their area. There are very few teams worldwide that are not named for the district, town or city that their stadium resides in. At the highest levels of British football only Arsenal famously buck the trend and it is arguable that had they stayed in their original area, they would have kept the early moniker of Woolwich Arsenal. Teams such as Manchester United changed their name to match their location deliberately in order to get a larger profile in the early days of football, while there is uproar when a move of just a few miles is mooted by a team even today. It is understandable, bearing in mind this close link between area and team, that many clubs worldwide gain their inspiration for their colours from their home area, whether from town coats of arms or state flags and below are some teams that have chosen this route.

Asante Kotoko	GHA	red/yellow - colours of Asante nation
Borussia Mönchengladbach	GER	white/black - from Prussian flag
Cagliari	ITA	red/blue - coat of arms
Ferencváros	HUN	green/white - coat of arms
Hamburger SV	GER	red/white - Hamburg's Hanseatic colours
FC Kaiserslautern	GER	red - city's colours
K. Sint-Truiden	BEL	yellow/blue - city's flag
Kyoto Sanga	JAP	purple - colour of Imperial City
RAEC Mons	BEL	red/white - city's colours
OGC Nice	FRA	black/red - coat of arms
Racing Santander	ESP	white/black/green - region's colours
Real Sociedad	ESP	blue/white - flag of San Sebastian
Real Valladolid	ESP	violet/white - city's colours
Red Star Belgrade	SER	red/white - Serbian flag
Rubin Kazan	RUS	red - region of Tatarstan's colours
Slavia Prague	CZR	red/white - flag of Czech Independence
Sporting Gijón	ESP	red/white/blue - figure on of city's flag
Toronto FC	CAN	red/white - Canadian flag (play in MLS)
Verona	ITA	yellow/blue - city's coat of arms
Werder Bremen	GER	green/white - flag of Saxony

NORWICH CITY

The Norfolk club originally played in blue and was known by the nickname 'The Citizens'. During the 1900s the city of Norwich was famous for the breeding

and exporting of canaries and the team were often being referred to by the nickname. In 1907 the team changed from blue and white to the yellow and green kit they wear to this day in reflection of their new nickname.

NOTTINGHAM FOREST

Forest had started their life as a football team wearing a set of red caps. In the late 19th century the Italian Giuseppe Garibaldi was a world renowned political figure and soldier who had just led his forces in the 1866 Austro-Prussian war. He was famed for his red shirted followers and he must have struck a chord with the board of Nottingham Forest as the club chose to wear a strip of 'Garibaldi Red' shirts in 1868, but this Garibaldi Red was darker than the colour worn today. (See p80).

The board's decision means that Forest have, apart from the lightening of the red, had essentially the same kit longer than any other club in the world. This famous kit has affected the strips that many clubs wear today (see p40) as Nottingham Forest's early influence on the game was widespread.

NOTTS COUNTY

The oldest club playing professionally in the world, having been formed in 1862, Notts County have played in their black and white stripes since switching from a chocolate and blue strip in 1890, although why this choice was made is unknown. Famously, Italy's most successful club side Juventus play in the same colours due to early connections with the Nottingham club (see p78). Indeed

to mark the opening of the Italians' new Juventus Stadium in September 2011, Juventus invited Notts County to play a friendly (which ended 1-1). County have,

in turn, invited Juventus for a return match at County's Meadow Lane in 2012 to celebrate County's 150th anniversary.

OLDHAM ATHLETIC

It is not known why Oldham wear blue, a colour they have played most of their history in. The Latics also wore a strip of red and white hoops in their earliest days and again briefly after the Second World War, possibly because shortages meant their blue kit was unavailable. This hooped kit was probably borrowed from Oldham's rugby club and a similar one has been brought back in recent years as an away kit.

OXFORD UNITED

Beginning their days as Headington United, the team possibly took its colours, orange and blue, from the town coat of arms which shows an orange ox and a blue river ford, although they sensibly ignored the black elephant, blue lion and especially the green beaver that also appear on the Oxford city coat of arms!

In the 1950s Headington took the short step from orange and blue to an amber and black kit and after becoming Oxford United in 1960, carried this colour combination on for a number of years before the black returned to blue in the 1970s.

PETERBOROUGH UNITED

The Supporters' Club of the 'Posh' originally bought Peterborough Utd's blue and white kit during an uncertain financial period of their early days. Blue and white are the predominant colours of the town's coat of arms and perhaps this is why the colours were chosen to replace the original green kit that had been donated to the struggling club. Over the years the shirts have been mainly all blue, though sometimes they have been styled with white sleeves.

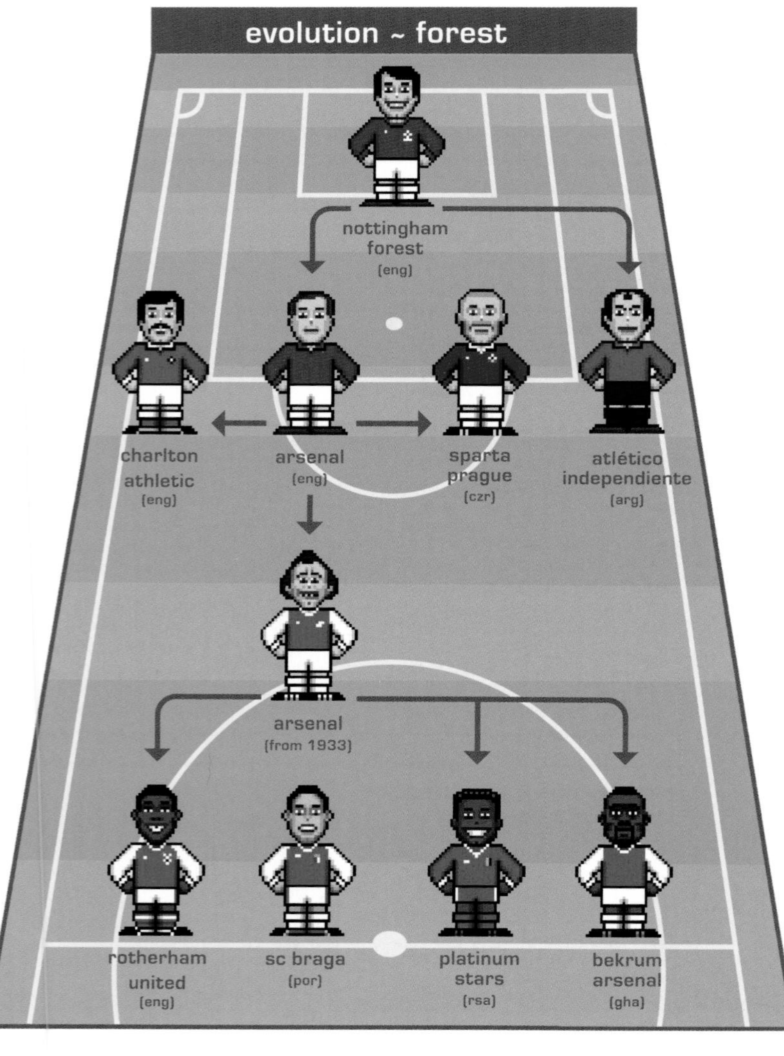
evolution ~ forest
nottingham
forest
(eng)
charlton
athletic
(eng)
arsenal
(eng)
sparta
prague
(czr)
atlético
independiente
(arg)
arsenal
(from 1933)
rotherham
united
(eng)
sc braga
(por)
platinum
stars
(rsa)
bekrum
arsenal
(gha)

PLYMOUTH ARGYLE

Plymouth Argyle seemed, unlike many other teams, not to consider green an unlucky colour (see Burnley p20) having always had green on their kit. The accepted reason for the colour choice is that green is the municipal colour of Plymouth. It has also been suggested that green may have been chosen to honour the famous (but probably apocryphal) story that Sir Francis Drake, prior to his finest hour against the Spanish Armada in 1588, had been playing a game of bowls on the green of Plymouth Hoe. Drake was supposed, on being warned of the approach of the Spanish fleet, to have remarked that there was plenty of time to "finish the game and still beat the Spaniard..."

PORTSMOUTH

Portsmouth began their days playing in pink and maroon, the colours of the city's trams. The city of Portsmouth has been an important naval base for many centuries and it is thought that the adoption of the navy blue was in honour of this.

PORT VALE

The team from the Burslem region of Stoke may have taken their black and white colours from the area's coat of arms. At one time the local area's crest was also the team badge and the club originally went by the name Burslem Port Vale before dropping the precursor's name in the early 20th century.

PRESTON NORTH END

The Lancashire club took much of their heritage from their local area. The club badge is the lamb of Preston's patron saint St.Wilfrid; while the town motto "Princeps Pacis" – Prince of Peace, represented as PP on the crest – as included on early team badges and altered to "Proud Preston" by the fans. The colours of the club also reflect the town's coat of arms of a white lamb on a blue background.

LOOK! THE ARSENAL CAPTAIN HAS DECIDED TO WEAR SHORT SLEEVES FOR TODAY'S GAME!
JVC

YES. AND BECAUSE OF THE CLUB'S TRADITION, THE REST OF THE TEAM HAVE TO WEAR SHORT SLEEVES TOO!
BRITISH
FOUN
JVC
JVC
JVC
BR

QUEENS PARK RANGERS

QPR once played in Oxford/ Cambridge halved shirts; they then went on to play in a green and white hooped combination similar to the famous Celtic kit. The fact that green was a supposed unlucky colour (see Burnley p20) meant that after a poor run of form in the 1920s a change was made to blue and white hoops, combining the new style with the old colours.

READING

Reading have always played in a blue and white combination. They originally played in stripes, changing to hoops after the numbering of shirts became compulsory in 1939 in the belief that numbers were easier to see against them. The colours are most likely taken from the coat of arms of the Berkshire town, although unlike other clubs, the team has never worn the arms as a team badge.

ROCHDALE

Rochdale originally wore black and white stripes in homage to Newcastle Utd. In 1949 they switched to a blue and white kit that they wore in various combinations over the years. The black and white would make a comeback in the 50s and 60s before the blue and white held sway for the later half of the 20th century.

In 2007 the club reverted to the black and white for their centenary season, and the next season they switched to an Inter Milan style kit, amalgamating the blue and white with the Newcastle inspired strip for their second century.

ROTHERHAM UNITED

According to club records Rotherham were looking at replacing their old kit in 1930. It had been suggested by the board that they change to green shirts (the predominant colour of the town's coat of arms) and the club were trying to get 500 fans to donate a shilling each as they were experiencing financial difficulties. Why red and white was chosen rather than green is a matter of

conjecture, though it has been suggested that they changed after a tour of Denmark that year, the Danish national team of course famously play in this colour combination. It is generally believed that they switched to their white-sleeved jerseys just after the Second World War to emulate the famous shirt style of the successful Arsenal team.

SCUNTHORPE UNITED

It is thought that Scunthorpe chose their colours to emulate either Aston Villa or Burnley. During the 60s and 70s they wore strips first of white and blue and then of all red after deciding claret and blue was old fashioned. The claret and blue returned in the 80s to coincide with a time of reinvention after a precarious period of relegations.

SHEFFIELD UNITED

Sheffield United took their colours from an old coat of arms of the family of Sheffield which was red and white. Whether this was also a choice because the already established Sheffield Wednesday played in blue and white and red and blue have always been natural opposites in football (see p48-49) is also a possibility.

SHEFFIELD WEDNESDAY

While rivals United took their colours from the Sheffield family crest, the City's blue and white may be the inspiration behind Wednesday's colours, though this is speculation. Wednesday's fans have built up some interesting superstitions around their kit; many older fans believe the team will have a poor season when they abandon the traditional evenly spaced stripe designs in favour of some broad or narrow stripe design, while other supporters prefer the shirt to have a blue central stripe, considering a white central stripe to be unlucky.

SHREWSBURY TOWN

Shrewsbury public school was one of the public schools that first championed association football. The football club, which was formed in 1886, took the blue and white colours of the school for their own. The white later changed to amber possibly echoing the colour of the three "Loggerheads" (Heraldic Leopards) on the town and team crest.

SOUTHAMPTON

The team nicknamed the Saints were linked to St Mary's Church and started playing in white with a red sash, possibly again an example of the link to purity (see Bury p21). The red and white stripes are said to have become the traditional Southampton kit after the south coast club signed some players from Stoke who brought their jerseys with them.

SOUTHEND UNITED

Southend Utd were formed when several teams came together to build a stronger club in the Essex town. They are said to have taken their colours as a reaction to Southend Athletic the largest local team who had worn red and they wanted the opposite. As the team was conceived in a meeting in the Blue Boar pub, this could have had some bearing on the choice of colours as well. In the 60s Southend tried to change to a dark navy blue; the FA however, refused as this clashed with the referee's kit. Now this rule has relaxed they play in this darker blue.

STOCKPORT COUNTY

Playing most of their seasons wearing the town's colours of blue and white, in 1979 they switched to the sky blue and white striped shirt and black shorts of the Argentina team that had just won the 78 World Cup. This proved to be a brief switch however, as they dropped the style when the Falklands conflict began in 1982. Since then, the darker blue and white has been worn in various combinations as the County strip.

STOKE CITY

After a period of almost as many name changes (Stoke Ramblers, Stoke and Stoke FC) as colour changes (blue and black hoops, amber and black stripes to name a few), the Staffordshire club settled down as Stoke City in 1925,

most likely taking their colours from the city's coat of arms, which is dominated by red and white. The crest was also the team badge until recent years.

SUNDERLAND

Reputedly Sunderland changed to red and white stripes as they were seen as more inspirational than an early blue kit

they wore. It has also been said that in their early days the Mackems ran into financial strife, even, it is said, raffling off a canary to keep the team going, while the strip was a gift from fellow north eastern team South Bank FC who were asked to help out.

SWANSEA CITY

Swansea City were formed in 1912 and took their colours from the already established Swansea Rugby Club that had been playing in white since 1874. It isn't recorded why the rugby team chose white but the link with the Swan of the city's name should probably not be discounted. The rugby team also had links with the city's cricket

team and this could explain why the colour synonymous with cricket was chosen.

SWINDON TOWN

Another club west country way that once played in green shirts, the Wiltshire club were unable to find a suitable green dye for a set of white shirts they had been given and settled on red instead. The green has returned as a minor trim detail in recent years for Swindon Town as obviously the availability

of dye has no longer become an issue in the manufacture of football shirts!

The Blues Vs. The Reds

The Blues	The Reds
Everton	Liverpool
Racing Club	Independiente
Manchester City	Manchester United
Stuttgarter Kickers	VfB Stuttgart
Bristol Rovers	Bristol City
Lazio	Roma
Sheffield Wednesday	Sheffield United
Inter Milan	AC Milan
Portsmouth	Southampton
Real Sociedad	Atletico Bilbao
Boca Juniors	River Plate
TSV Munchen 1860	Bayern Munich
QPR	Brentford
Levski Sofia	CSKA Sofia
IFK Goteborg	Orgyte IS

The Blues vs The Reds

There is something undeniably classic about a game of football between a team playing in blue versus a team in red. Whether the green of the pitch is bathed in sun for a May cup final or it's a rainy December mid-week game under the floodlights, when the teams are wearing red and blue it just adds something. Numerous TV pundits over the years have commented on it and if you're looking to buy a table football game or a Subbuteo set they will invariably come with a blue and red team as standard.

It seems, as the illustration to the left shows, that an out of proportion amount of local derbies from Merseyside to Buenos Aires are contested between teams of red and blue. So have we only got a soft spot for the blues v the reds because everyone, including the neutral, loves a derby? Or did teams consciously choose red because their local rival wore blue? There is evidence that some teams did just that; Sheffield Utd chose red after the already established Sheffield Wednesday had laid claim to blue and Southend Utd chose blue, as a local team was known for wearing red too. This is not just an English phenomenon with Italy's famous Inter Milan, who were formed in a breakaway move from AC Milan, choosing blue almost to underline their differences.

Of course fierce rivalries are played out in other colours; the East Anglian derby is contested between Ipswich's blue and Norwich's yellow, while the bitter green and white vs blue of the Glasgow derby is perhaps one of the world's most famous, but you can't get away from it, red and blue, colours that aren't polar opposites anywhere else clash wonderfully on derby day.

So where do your loyalties lie? Are you a red or a blue?

TORQUAY UNITED

Torquay started their days playing in a black and white striped kit; romantically they changed in 1954 to a strip of gold shirts to represent the sun and sand with blue shorts for the sea and skies of the Devon seaside resort. The colours have been worn in many styles since the original gold with blue sleeves, with blue as the major

colour, striped kits although the style of all gold with blue trim has been the favourite.

TOTTENHAM HOTSPUR

Spurs changed to the colour combination of white shirts and blue shorts a decade after and in emulation of the successful Preston North End team who had achieved the league and cup double in 1889.

In European competitions Spurs have often worn an all-white kit, which was instigated by

60s manager Bill Nicholson in tribute to the multiple conquerors of Europe Real Madrid (right).

TRANMERE ROVERS

When manager Dave Russell was appointed in 1961 he initiated

the change to the all-white kit, saying 'Liverpool are red, Everton are blue and now, Tranmere are all white.' It is also widely believed Russell was influenced by Real Madrid's famous all-white strip (right).

WALSALL

The West Midlands club is another team that briefly played in Aston

Villa's colours (in the 1920s and 1950s). Their more familiar kit of red and white came from their precursor club Walsall Swifts who merged with Walsall Town to form first Walsall Town Swifts before completing the journey by changing their name to plain Walsall in 1893.

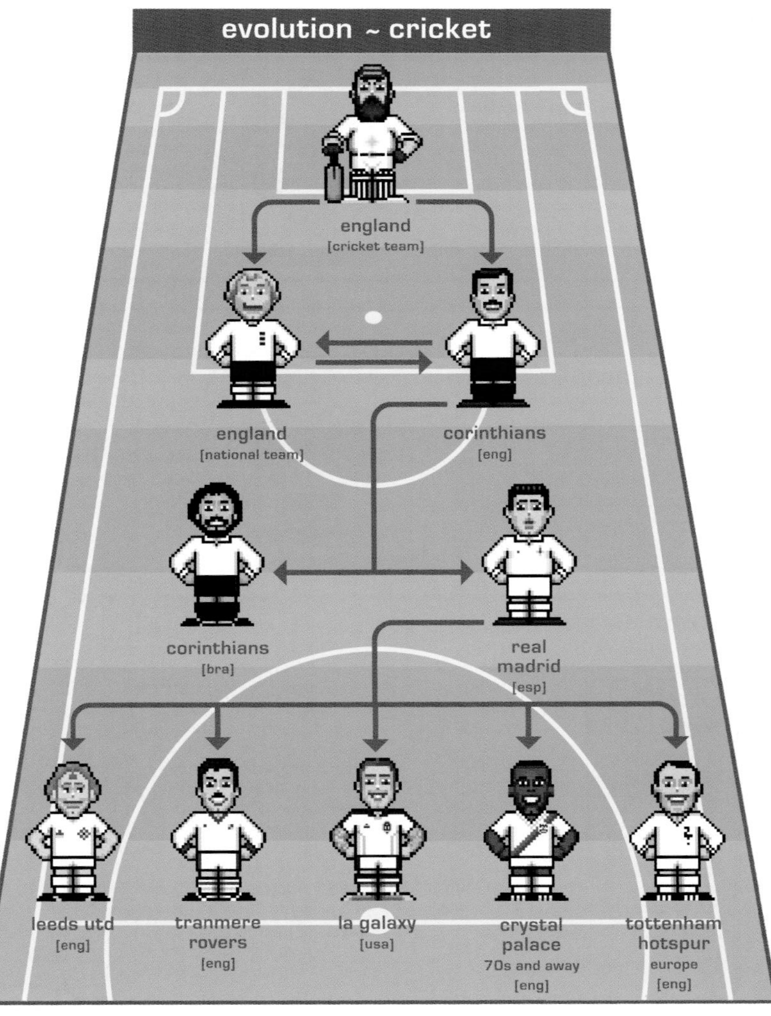
evolution ~ cricket
england
[cricket team]
england
[national team]
corinthians
[eng]
corinthians
[bra]
real
madrid
[esp]
leeds utd
[eng]
tranmere
rovers
[eng]
la galaxy
[usa]
crystal
palace
70s and away
[eng]
tottenham
hotspur
europe
[eng]

WATFORD

Having played in many different early kits including a bizarre green, red and yellow-hooped affair, Watford settled into yellow and black strips in the 60s. This led to the nickname 'The Hornets'. A red hornet later became the team badge and in the 70s this red was incorporated as part of the

club's colours, becoming synonymous with the club during their hey day in the 1980s with Elton John and Graham Taylor's famous team.

WEST BROMWICH ALBION

The Midlands club had tried lots of different colour combinations including the striped kit they wear today. In 1889 they wore a new strip with jerseys of blue and red, however this proved unpopular, the players being wolf whistled and called 'Nigger Minstrels' as the colours were similar to those worn by white music hall artists who performed

songs with blackened faces. In response to this Albion switched to the older colour scheme of blue and white stripes and this time the combination stuck.

WEST HAM UNITED

Formed originally as the works team of the Thames Ironworks

shipbuilding firm, West Ham's first strip was the dark blue of the firm's owner Arnold Hill's school Oxford. In their early days the Ironworks also played in a strip consisting of sky blue shirts, white shorts and red socks sometimes with a red sash tied round the waist. This kit is most likely to have come from a local club, Old Castle Swifts, which had folded with many of the players joining Thames Ironworks and bringing their shirts with them, although some sources say this combination came from the shipbuilding firm's colours.

Thames Ironworks became West Ham United when they went professional. West Ham are said to have gained the Villa-style strip when William Dove, a professional sprinter was challenged, at a fair in Birmingham, to a race against four Villa players. The players wagered money that one of them would win. Dove won the race, but the Villa players were unable to pay. One

of the Villa men, however, was responsible for washing the team's kit and offered a complete side's strip to Dove in payment. The Aston Villa player subsequently reported to his club that the kit had gone missing. Dove, as well as being a coach at West Ham, also had his son Charlie at the club as a player and he passed the kit over to the club.

In recent years West Ham have committed to a three-way rotation of away kits; the sky blue of the 60s (based on the original Swifts kit), the dark blue of the Ironworks kit and largely white kits which are associated with the 1980 cup final victory over Arsenal.

WIGAN ATHLETIC

After the Second World War, Wigan who had up till then played in red and white needed a new kit, they were forced to use blue as this was the only colour a local supplier had in stock in a post-war Britain with rationing still in place. Since then, Wigan Athletic have used various combinations of blue and white.

AFC WIMBLEDON

After the team that had been Wimbledon relocated to Milton Keynes and became the MK Dons (see page 34), AFC Wimbledon was formed by supporters incensed at the move. The new team obviously took the colours of the previous club, who had in turn taken their most famous colour combination of blue and yellow from the coat of arms of the borough of Wimbledon.

WOLVERHAMPTON WANDERERS

Wolves' famous 'old gold' and black strip comes from the municipal colours of Wolverhampton, which in turn represent the town's motto 'Out of Darkness Cometh Light'. The saying can be traced back to Mayan times, but was used by the council to relate to the industrial revolution when Wolverhampton was, indeed, a centre of great industry. The combination that has changed little since the 1930s is one of the most distinctive in English football.

WREXHAM

Though there is no firm evidence, the best guess for Wrexham's post-war choice of a change to red shirts is the link with Wales, red being the traditional national colour. If this was not the original reason it seems now to represent this link, the introduction of green as trim in recent years tends to confirm this as this is the third colour (along with the white, which the team use

for their shorts) that appears on the Welsh flag. The team's badge is also replete with Welsh imagery; being red, white and green, showing two Red Dragons and the Prince of Wales's feathers.

WYCOMBE WANDERERS

Many early teams chose to play in the varsity colours of Oxford or Cambridge, as the public schools were a source of many of the first players of the game. Wycombe chose both light and dark blues playing in halves, stripes, quartered and plain versions before the quarters returned for good in the 90s. Like Bristol Rovers

the location of the dark and light blue quarters switches on the shirt, often being opposite to the illustration shown.

YEOVIL TOWN

Like many teams from the west of England Yeovil wear green, but

unlike most they haven't dismissed the shirts because of green's supposed links with bad luck. (See Burnley p20.) The colours of the club came from the Yeovil Casuals, a forefather of the modern club.

YORK CITY

York chose red as a team colour after their previous chocolate and

cream strip led to many colour clashes with other teams. As well as occasionally changing the red for maroon for a period in the 70s and once in recent years, York had a unique strip with a large 'Y' on the front of their shirt.

And now a late result...

FLEETWOOD TOWN
You'd be excused for thinking that the team known as the 'Cod Army' who were promoted to the Football League for the first time in their history in 2012 get their colours and kit styling from Arsenal, especially as the Lancashire club's home ground is called Highbury! In fact the colours go back to 1919, pre-dating the North London club, because of Fleetwood's close links with a local Trawler company whose corporate colours they adopted.

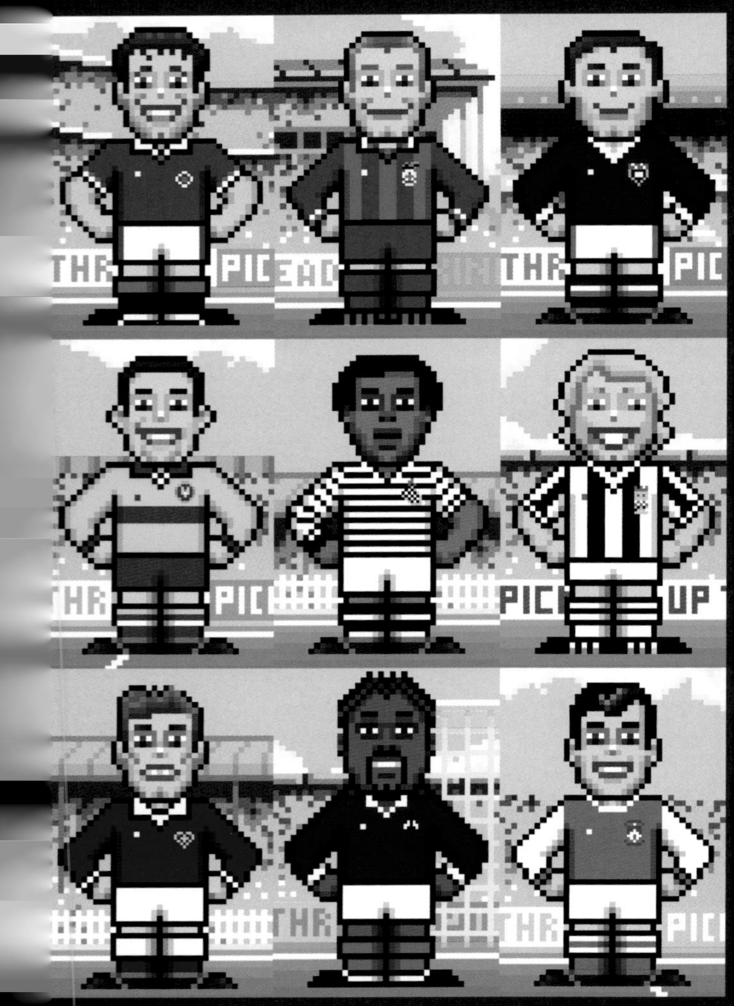

Scottish Club Teams

ABERDEEN

Aberdeen formed in 1903 playing in a strip of black and gold stripes

until 1939, before changing to their now famous red and white. The club from Pittodrie Stadium changed to the colours they still wear today to reflect the red and silver of the official arms of the city of Aberdeen.

ARBROATH

The team most famous for the British record win of 36 goals to nil against

Bon Accord in the Scottish Cup of 1885 get their claret shirts from the red sandstone of the area; though they also go by the nickname of the 'Red Lichties' after the navigation lights used by the local fishing fleet.

CELTIC

The Glasgow club were formed in 1887 by Brother Walfrid, an Irish Catholic priest who was working with the Irish community of Glasgow after being inspired

by the Edinburgh club Hibernian. Like many other Scottish clubs with Irish roots, Hibernian included, Celtic chose the colours of green and white, colours synonymous with their homeland. Having started their playing days playing mostly in striped shirts, the famous hooped style is thought to come from the style of one of Hibernian's early kits.

DUNDEE

Dundee was formed by the merger of local teams East End and Our Boys. In their first season they alternated between the striped shirts of East End and navy blue of Our Boys before settling on the navy blue similar to the national team's colours.

DUNDEE UNITED

Originally wearing all white United played in the 60s in the North American Soccer League (NASL) during the summer, wearing the American sounding 'columbia blue and burnt orange' as the Dallas Tornadoes;

alongside other teams including Stoke City (Cleveland Stokers), Wolves (Los Angeles Wolves), Sunderland (Vancouver Royal Canadians) and Aberdeen (Washington Whips). In 1969 United took these colours back home as their regular kit, but as blue was the colour of their city rivals Dundee they replaced it with black.

DUNFERMLINE ATHLETIC

Why the Fife team wear black and white stripes is unfortunately unknown. The parallel stripes are believed by some to give them their nickname 'The Pars', though it has been suggested this comes from the early team's ability to put away the odd pint and is a derivation of 'Paralytics!'

FALKIRK

As with many teams in Scotland, Falkirk wear the national colours. The navy blue shirts and white shorts have often been accompanied by red socks (though navy and white are also used), the same combination used by the national team (See p104).

HEART OF MIDLOTHIAN

Hearts once turned out in a jersey of white, red and blue hoops.

Depending on what source you believe either the shirt was unpopular with players due to their cost or the colours ran together in the wash. Whatever the reason maroon became Hearts' colours from 1877.

HIBERNIAN

Ireland provided the inspiration for the green and white colours of Hibernian. The Edinburgh club was formed in 1874 by Catholic Irish immigrants, while the club's name comes from the Latin name for Ireland. Hibs wore plain green shirts until the late 1930s when the white

sleeves which have become a mainstay of the club's shirt was introduced.

INVERNESS CALEDONIAN THISTLE

The merger of Inverness Thistle and Caledonian in 1994 was instigated to take advantage of a re-organisation of the Scottish league and a move to take one of the two extra places that were to be created. The new league club took on the red of Inverness Thistle and the blue of Caledonian as the basis of its new kit.

KILMARNOCK

The Ayrshire team started their playing days wearing a plain dark blue shirt similar to the national team. This changed to a more royal blue and, matched with white, the style to hoops. They have also worn stripes, which were, in 1960, an attempt to change the club's fortunes after they finished runners-up in both league and cup. This didn't do much good, however, as the next year they also finished league runners-up. However they finally won the league in 1965 wearing stripes. Since then plain blue, white, and hoops have been used, but stripes have become the norm.

LIVINGSTON

Livingston started out as Ferranti Thistle, the works team of electronics manufacturers Ferranti and playing in the Edinburgh firm's colours, before becoming Meadowbank Thistle in 1974 and joining the restructured Scottish league. In 1995 financial difficulties led to the club relocating to Livingston with the new club keeping the colours of Thistle.

MOTHERWELL

In another case of a team trying to emulate a bigger team's success Motherwell took their colours from English club Bradford City in 1913, who had won the FA Cup in 1911. Over the years, Motherwell have made the colours their own with the amber coming to dominate the claret on their home kit.

PARTICK THISTLE

Partick Thistle who, despite their name, haven't played in the Partick area of Glasgow since 1908, residing in the Maryhill area, originally played in navy but switched to a hooped red and yellow strip with black shorts. This combination was probably taken up after Thistle borrowed a set of jerseys from the local rugby team, West of Scotland. The colours have been worn in many combinations, mainly hoops and stripes, but also plain over the years.

QUEEN'S PARK

Queen's Park has an impressive heritage, being the first major power in Scottish football. In fact the first Scotland team ran out in the 1872 game against England in Glasgow wearing the navy shirts, white shorts and red and white hooped socks that they still wear today, basically because all eleven players were from Queen's Park and this was their club strip. While the national team stuck with this colour combination, Queen's Park changed to a black and white hooped combination when they entered their new stadium in 1873.

RANGERS

The Glasgow club made a conscious decision to play in a lighter blue than the many other Scottish teams that played in a blue closer to that seen on the cross of St Andrew. Over time the colour became a more Unionist royal blue and when joined by the white shorts and red trim the sectarian links that run through football in Glasgow can clearly be seen. Interestingly, this fairly obvious combination has been joined by black socks for most of Ranger's history, the reason for which is unknown.

Rangers have followed their colour scheme through to their away kits which for the majority of their history have been largely red or white though on a couple of occasions orange has been chosen, a clear link with their Unionist roots and the Orange Order which still holds sway in many parts of Protestant Glasgow.

OH NO! HE'S BEEN SHOWN THE RED CARD!
HE SHOULD HAVE HEEDED THE WARNING THAT A YELLOW CARD IS INTENDED TO SIGNAL!

RAITH ROVERS

The team from Kirkcaldy have for large parts of their history worn

royal blue; however by far their favoured shade has, like many other Scottish teams, been a strip based on the national colours of navy shirts and white shorts with occasional red trim reminiscent of the Scottish national team (see p104). Though they have mainly worn a plain shirt in navy they have at times worn different styles including a halved kit in 2008 to celebrate their 125th anniversary.

ROSS COUNTY

The Highland team wear the colour combination of navy shirts with

white shorts and either red, white or navy socks. This is based, like many other Scottish teams, on the famous combination of the national team (see p104).

ST JOHNSTONE

The Perth team probably take their colours from the Scottish Saltire.

Certainly the blue and white of their strip is echoed in the club's traditional badge of a lamb cradling the flag of St Andrew.

ST MIRREN

There is some dispute as to why the colours black and white were chosen for the team from Paisley. The most popular theories are...

That the Cluniac Monks who founded Paisley Abbey wore black and white robes.

That the colours may have come from when Paisley used to play host to an annual charity match between chimney sweeps (represented by the black soot) and bakers (white flour).

Or finally that they come from the River Cart which run through Paisley and which splits into the smaller rivers the White Cart and Black Cart.

THE REFEREE

In the early days of football it was more common for referees to wear a blazer than a shirt or jersey. Traditionally the referee wore the neutral colour of black, unless one of the teams was wearing a very dark jersey, such as Scotland, in which case the referee would wear another colour (usually red) to distinguish themselves from the teams.

Commercialism and the increasing power of TV in the 80s and 90s meant there was much more variation in teams' colours and new colours for the officials were introduced: burgundy, yellow and white joined black at the 1994 World Cup finals in the USA, while green became an alternative in the English Premier League.

Today at international level FIFA's referees and their assistants wear black, red, yellow or blue, while individual associations can use many more colours, the Italian league for example uses fluorescent yellow.

RED AND YELLOW CARDS

The use of the red and yellow card system came about after the 1966 World Cup quarter final between England and Argentina. The bad tempered game was almost abandoned when Argentine captain Rattín refused to leave the pitch after being sent-off by German referee Rudolf Kreitlein. After the game, reports in newspapers claimed that the referee had booked England defender Jack Charlton, a fact that had got lost in the confusion of the game. The Head of Referees at the World Cup, Ken Aston, driving after the game from Wembley to the FA's headquarters at Lancaster Gate experienced a journey interrupted by many sets of traffic lights. Aston realised that a colour coding system similar to the one used by traffic lights, amber for steady and red for stop, would avoid such confusion and work in international football where language could be a barrier.

The cards were first used at the 1970 World Cup in Mexico, the first yellow was shown in a game between Mexico and the Soviet Union (five players were booked but there is no record of who was first). The first red was shown to Carlos Caszely of Chile at the 1974 tournament.

European & World Club Teams

AC MILAN (Italy)

The famous Italian side owes its foundation to the early English exporters of the game to Italy; indeed they still keep the English spelling of Milan in honour of English founders rather than using the Italian name 'Milano'.

This English heritage led also to the team's colours and one of their nicknames, 'The Devils', which John Foot recounts in his book 'Calcio': "The team's most influential early player was [Englishman] Herbert Kiplin... he chose the team's red-and-black shirts. Relatives of Kiplin argue that it was his Protestantism, in a Catholic country, which led to the epithet. Kiplin is supposed to have said that our 'shirts must be red

because we are devils. Let's put in some black to give everyone a fright.'"

AC Milan's official line shifts the emphasis slightly with their website claiming the red represents the team's "fire", rather than Kiplin's more satanic metaphor.

Like all Italian teams Milan also have a nickname that is centred around their colours; possibly the most famous of the Italian colour nicknames, they are referred to as the 'Rossoneri' from the Italian words for red and black. (See p74-75).

AEK ATHENS (Greece)

Refugees from Turkish Constantinople formed AEK in the Greek capital in 1924. Many of these refugees had links with the Constantinople club Pera, who had played in yellow and black, so the colours were adopted by their new team. AEK have worn many combinations of the colours including

hoops, stripes and in the 90s a couple of kits with the club's double-headed eagle crest splashed across it.

ALIANZA LIMA (Peru)

The oldest team in Peru, Alianza take their traditional striped kit of blue and white stripes with black shorts from the colours of the racing stables that hosted their first games.

During every October, as a tribute to the main Catholic festival in Peru, Alianza switch to

the traditional Catholic Church's colour, sporting a strip of purple and white stripes, with purple shorts and socks.

AJAX (Netherlands)

When the Amsterdam club were promoted to the Dutch top division in 1911, they played in the same colours as Sparta Rotterdam, all-black. At that time there was a rule that no two teams could play in the same kit in the Dutch league. Ajax being the new boys changed to the now famous white with a single thick red central stripe, a unique

style that the 70s team of Cruyff and Neeskens made so famous that it is now referred to as the 'Ajax' style when seen on other kits worldwide.

ANDERLECHT (Belgium)

There is a little uncertainty why Belgium's most successful team chose purple and white as its colours. Founder Charles Roos is believed to have chosen the colours for one of two reasons: the first is the club's strong links with the

Catholic Church, which traditionally uses purple in many of its vestments. Anderlecht took many of their best players from the Catholic institute Saint-Nicholas and played their first game in 1908 against the church team Saint-Georges. The other possible inspiration for Charles Roos that has sometimes been quoted was a famous flower parade in Anderlecht that Princess Elisabeth (Queen Consort of Albert I of Belgium) took part in; her coach was decorated in purple and white orchids which matched her dress. The team has strong links to the monarchy, their full title being Royal Sporting Club Anderlecht.

ATHLETIC BILBAO (Spain)

As the English and Scottish exporters of football had strong connections in Spain, it was almost inevitable that they would have a great deal of influence on the development of Spanish teams' colours. The fiercely independent Basque region soon had its standard bearing teams, among them Athletic Bilbao. It is said their

colours come from a visit to London in 1909 by student Juan Elorduy who was asked to buy a new set of shirts. He was unable to find enough, but waiting for the

ship back home in Southampton he realised that the Saint's colours matched the colours of Bilbao's flag, and bought fifty shirts.

There is also a more pragmatic reason for the choice of colours: the same combination of red and white stripes was used, in Spain, for the cloth of mattresses. This cloth was available pre-dyed and was cheap and easy to make into football shirts.

CLUB ATLÉTICO INDEPENDIENTE (Argentina)

After the club president, Aristides Langone saw Nottingham Forest play in a 1905 friendly match in Argentina, he is said to have proclaimed: "I want these colours for Independiente, Red Devils seem real!" The club's original shirt of blue and white halves became their away kit, interestingly keeping the old blue crest on it to this day.

ATLÉTICO MADRID (Spain)

The Madrid club was formed by students of Bilbao and was originally a subsidiary of Athletic Bilbao, hence the team colours' close resemblance to the Basque club. The first set of shirts are said to have been left-overs from Juan Elorduy's trip to England (see p69) The new team also took advantage of the cheap mattress cloth available in Spain and this has led to their nickname Los Colchoneros (The Mattress Makers).

BARCELONA (Spain)

The world-famous team from Spain's Catalan region have worn their strip of blue and red stripes since their earliest days. The team was formed in 1899 by a mix of Swiss, English and Catalonians. There are several popular theories as to why the colours were chosen listed below.

The most popular reason amongst Barça fans is that the colours were chosen by Swiss co-founder Hans Kamper and are the colours of his home-town team FC Basel.

While Arthur Witty, the son of the first president,

claimed he chose the colours as they were those of his Liverpool school, Merchant Taylors.

Or that the colours were chosen in support of the French revolution and the colours of Robespierre's First Republic; a conscious political snub, that came from the complicated world of Spanish politics, from the Catalonian's to Madrid.

Strangely some believe the colours are based on the colours of the blue and red accountancy pencils that were popular in Spain at that time.

Finally it is said that the colours come from sashes the players played in from before they could afford kits of their own.

BAYERN MUNICH (Germany)

Bayern, Germany's most successful club, play in the red, white and occasionally blue associated with their home state of Bavaria. They also wear a distinct kit for games outside their domestic league, such as the Champions League; in 2009 this was all-white, for 2011 all-dark blue.

During the 1980s and 90s Bayern used a unique 'Brazil' yellow and blue away kit when they were playing fellow Bundesliga team Kaiserslautern; this was a superstition that came about because Bayern found it hard to win there.

BELGRANO DE CÓRDOBA (Argentina)

The team from the city of Córdoba are named after the famous Argentinean hero Manuel Belgrano, an economist, political figure, lawyer and soldier. Involved in the Argentinean War of Independence, Belgrano also designed the flag of Argentina and the club take their team's colours from this in tribute to him. (See p80).

BOCA JUNIORS (Argentina)

The Argentinean club, who name Diego Maradona and Carlos Tevez amongst their famous ex-players, gained their blue and yellow kit in unusual circumstances. In 1906 Boca played in unpopular black and white stripes and so switched to light blue, before a game with fellow Buenos Aires rivals Nottingham de Almagro, whose kit was very

similar. The teams made a bet: whoever won would continue to use the sky blue. Boca lost and returned to using their unpopular black and white jersey. The next year the team still wanted new colours, but still indecision reigned on what those colours should be. Club president Juan Brichetto came up with a novel solution: he had the idea of going to the port of La Boca and using the colours of the flag of the first boat that passed. His idea was accepted and a group of club officials headed for the port. The first boat to appear was the freighter *Drottning* [Queen] *Sophia*, whose Swedish blue and gold colours are used to this day. Their fans must thank their stars it wasn't a Greenpeace boat!

BORUSSIA DORTMUND (Germany)

One of Germany's most successful clubs, Dortmund was founded in 1909 by young footballers of church team Trinity Youth, who were fed up with a harsh local pastor who was dictating much of the activities of the church side. Their first jersey was blue and white striped and had a diagonal red sash. In 1913, after the club merged with two others, the traditional yellow and black strip was chosen. Worn in many styles including, plain, hoops and striped, in recent years the yellow has become more fluorescent.

BOTAFOGO (Brazil)

The team's colours come from the first star seen in the night sky, known in Brazil as Estrela Solitária (the Lone Star). In actual fact it is the planet Venus, but this minor point hasn't worried the Rio club who also wear the star as their team crest.

SC BRAGA (Portugal)

Braga's colours are famously based on those of Arsenal. This was either after the then coach Jozef Szabo was impressed with Arsenal's style of play or at the behest of chairman José Antunes Guimarães. Braga is nicknamed Arsenal do Minho (Arsenal of the [River] Minho) and have even named their youth team Arsenal do Braga.

CHICAGO FIRE (USA)

The MLS team is named after the Great Chicago Fire of 1871 that was apocryphally started by a cow kicking over a lantern. The kit's styling continues this link with the thick band being based on the style of a fireman's jacket. The colours match the red with white band scheme of the Chicago firetrucks and the team's crest completes the branding, being based on the Chicago Fire Department's logo.

COLORADO RAPIDS (USA)

A Rapids press release said 'The burgundy and sky blue tones that reign in the team's new identity are a continuation of the common DNA that runs through the identities of the other sports entities in the KSE family.' Essentially, the owner Stan Kroenke is building up a brand colour for his teams, which include the Colorado Avalanche ice hockey team. Fans of Arsenal, of whom Kroenke is a major shareholder, shouldn't be too worried about the Gunners turning out in claret and blue though, as he has kept the LA Rams' traditional colours since taking them over in 1995.

DYNAMO MOSCOW (Russia)

Dynamo has its roots in the works team of the Morozow Mille and were set up in 1887 by the English general manger, Harry Charnock, becoming Dynamo Moscow in 1923 at the behest of Felix Dzerzhinsky, the notorious head of the Soviet secret police, the Cheka. During the era of the Soviet Union, Dynamo, who were run by Dzerzhinsky's Ministry of the Interior, claimed their blue and white colours were inspired by the two elements man could not live without, namely water and air. The truth is Charnock had chosen the colours (though not the distinctive halved style) of the English team he supported, Blackburn Rovers.

The Italians

The Italians were one of the first countries outside of Britain to embrace the game of football. Colours are sacrosanct in Italy, with most teams not going through a period of change to the colours that their British counterparts did in their early years (Parma being a notable exception). This is followed through to the colour nicknames that all Italian teams have, and by which they are often referred to. Some of the most well known are listed below.

As further decoration to Italian shirts, the winners of the Italian championship bear 'lo Scudetto' (the little shield) a shield in the red, white and green of the Italian flag, a practice started in 1924 by Genoa to celebrate their victory. Similarly the winners of the Italian Cup competition, the 'Coppa Italia' wear a similarly coloured roundel akin to those seen on military aircraft.*

Italian teams also get to wear 'The Golden Star of Sports Excellence' on their shirt for every ten championship wins; so far Juventus have two stars, (though this is in dispute because of recent match fixing scandals) Inter and AC Milan have one each, while poor old Genoa have no stars, having been stuck on nine league titles since that win in 1924!

"Rossoneri"	The red & blacks	AC Milan
"La Viola"	The purple team	Fiorentina
"I Rossoblu"	The red & blues	Genoa
"Nerazzuri"	The black & blues	Internazionale
"I Bianconeri"	The black & whites	Juventus
"Biancocelesti"	The white & sky blues	SS Lazio
"Rosanero"	The pink & blacks	Palermo
"Gialloblu"	The yellow & blues	Parma
"I Giallorossi"	The yellow & reds	AS Roma
"I Blucerchiati"	The blue ringed	Sampdoria
"I Granata"	The clarets	Torino

* In England the champions get to wear a gold Premier League badge the next season as opposed to the normal blue, whilst Rangers in Scotland use the one star equals ten titles system. The star is used in England to represent anything from FA Cup wins (Bury) to European titles (Aston Villa & Nottingham Forest) and in world football to represent significant trophies (usually World Cups).

"i bianconeri"
[black and whites]
juventus
"rossoneri"
[red and black]
ac milan
"nerazzuri "
[black and blue]
internazionale
ITALIA

ENOSIS NEON PARALIMNI (Cyprus)

Anastasis and Jimmy Alexandrou ran a Cypriot restaurant in London. A regular patron and friend was West Ham legend Bobby Moore, who sent a set of Hammers shirts and shorts to Cyprus when Enosis needed a new kit, and they have used the colour combination ever since.

ESPANYOL (Spain)

The Spanish club wear their colours in honour of the Italian Admiral Roger de Lluria who was a 13th century Commander of the fleet of Aragon during the War of the Sicilian Vespers. A war hero on a par with Nelson to the Spanish, he was infamous for his devastating defeats of his enemies (see p81).

FENERBAHÇE (Turkey)

The then Sultan of Turkey had forbidden his subjects to indulge themselves in the 'English game', however in 1907 a group of keen footballers set up the club. A lighthouse situated on the Fenerbahçe cape was a focal point for the club, being its first crest while the team's colours of yellow and white came from the daffodils

around the lighthouse. The original kits were yellow and white stripes. Although the white stripes have since been replaced with navy, white has remained as the colour of the shorts.

AFC FIORENTINA (Italy)

The distinctive purple kit of the team from Florence was adopted in 1928. Tradition has it that the colour came from an accident after the old red and white kit was washed in the river and the colours ran.

FIRST VIENNA (Austria)

Rampaging Scottish gardeners

playing football in the gardens of Nathaniel Anselm von Rothschild led to much damage to the flowerbeds. To avoid further destruction,

Rothschild gave them a pasture nearby and a set of former jockeys' jerseys in the blue and yellow colour of his riding stable. The team of gardeners later became First Vienna.

GALATASARAY (Turkey)

The area of Galatasaray was, according to legend, founded when Bayezid, a 15th century Ottoman Sultan, became a guest of an old wise man, Gül Baba. The wise man presented the Sultan with two roses, one red and one yellow. The Sultan, impressed by this gesture, offered the wise man whatever he wished for. Gül Baba showed him a piece of land overlooking the Bosphorus, and asked him to build a school there. The club chose the colours of the roses for their team (see p81).

GRASSHOPPER CLUB ZÜRICH (Switzerland)

One of the pivotal figures in the founding of Grasshopper in 1886 was Englishman Tom Griffiths. As a Blackburn fan he introduced the famous blue and white halved kit to the new Swiss team. At the time Blackburn wore the blue on the right of their kit (it has been on the left since 1935) whereas Grasshopper still have it on the right of their shirts to this day.

IFK GOTHENBURG (Sweden)

The Idrottsföreningen Kamraterna (Sporting Society of Comrades) is an organisation that has set up many sporting clubs in Sweden and other Northern European countries. The colours of the organisation are blue and white representing loyalty and innocence. Most IFK clubs including IFK Göteborg play in a combination of blue and white; IFK Mora of Sweden and IFK Vasa of Finland are further instances of this. An IFK team that wants to play in another colour, such as Swedish team IFK Malmo who play in yellow, must get a special permit in order to do so.

INTER MILAN (Italy)

Breakaway members of AC Milan formed the Football Club Internazionale Milano in 1908, as at the time AC only allowed Italian players. The new team wanted to be open to all nationalities and thus chose the name Internazionale and the colours black to represent the night and blue, (the opposite of AC's red) to represent the sky. In 1928, Inter's name and policy of embracing foreigners fell foul of Mussolini's Fascists. The club was forcibly merged with another Milan club, Unione Sportiva Milanese, and renamed Ambrosiana SS Milano after

the city's patron saint. The kit was changed to the flag of Milan (a red cross on white). After the Fascists' fall, the club reverted to their original name and colours. The period has not been forgotten; in 2008 Inter wore a red cross on their away shirt to celebrate their centenary and since then as their third kit.

JUVENTUS (Italy)

The most successful team in the history of Italian football originally played in pink shirts with a black tie after being sent the wrong shirts. After continual washing the shirts faded and in 1903 they needed a new set. The team asked one of their players, Englishman John Savage, to see if he could get some shirts from England that could better withstand the demands of football. Savage turned to a friend in Nottingham who sent a set of the black and white

striped shirts of Notts County to the Turin club. Juve considered the colour combination to be both powerful and aggressive and have worn the shirts ever since. Today, Juve wear a more durable version of the pink shirt as their away kit.

SS LAZIO (Italy)

The famous Rome club started its days as a club that played many other sports as well as football. To reflect this the chosen colours were inspired by the Olympic movement ideals with Lazio taking their colours from the flag of the founders of the Olympics, Greece. Originally playing

with sky blue and white quartered shirts the plain sky blue became the favoured style, though a striped kit is also sometimes worn.

RC LENS (France)

Legend has it that the French team's president Pierre Moglia chose the colours after being told that the ruins of the Saint-Léger Church he was walking past were the last remains of Spanish occupation in 1648, so he adopted the colours of the Spanish flag for his team. An alternative version is the colours symbolise the local coal mining industry; red for the blood of the miners, gold to represent the value of the coal.

LA GALAXY (USA)

It is not often that one player can change the colours of the whole club, but this was the case for LA Galaxy. The original kit of the MLS team in 1996 was a horrific black and teal-green halved affair, with red trim and a weird graphic resembling yellow lightning bolts. They then switched to a teal-green kit with a gold sash and this became their standard kit until 2007. Then David Beckham came. The signing of the world's most famous sportsman prompted a mid-season change of strip and team crest. The new colours were chosen as all-white to resemble Beckham's previous club, Real Madrid, and was part of an overall bid by Galaxy, the MLS and Beckham to increase the prestige of Association Football in the US (see p51).

AS MONACO (France)

The French Riviera's sovereign city-state has always been more famous for the red of Ferrari and black and white chequered flags seen when hosting the jewel in the crown event of the Formula 1 season. This iconic event was challenged in the 70s and 80s as the teams of Lucien Leduc and Arsène Wenger brought success to Monaco. Unsurprisingly the team take the colours of the Principality for their own with Les Rouge et Blancs (The Red & Whites) being worn in a striking diagonal pattern.

GIUSEPPE GARIBALDI Rebel Leader
(1807-1882) Italian national hero. A political and military figure, he was a member of the red shirted Carbonari Italian Patriots Revolutionaries.

GERALD OAKLEY Earl of Cadogan
(1869-1933) British peer and soldier, who saw service in the Boer War, 6th Earl of Cadogan.

JOSÉ DE SAN MARTIN General (1778-1850)
Argentinean political leader and general in the struggle for South America's independence from Spain, famed for his red jacketed Grenadiers.

MANUEL BELGRANO Lawyer (1770-1820)
Economist, political figure, lawyer and soldier. Involved in the Argentinean War of Independence and designed the flag of Argentina.

People whose achievements have led clubs to adopt a colour associated with them.

ROGER DE LLÚRIA Admiral (1245-1305) Commander of the fleet of Aragon during the War of the Sicilian Vespers. Infamous for his devastating defeats of his enemies.

GEORGE STEPHENSON Engineer (1781-1848) Known as the "Father of the Railways". He built the first public railway line and the famous "Rocket" steam train.

GÜL BABA Wise Man (? -1541) Ottoman poet and companion of Sultan Suleiman the Magnificent. Known as the "Father of Roses".

WILLIAM OF ORANGE Holy Rom. Emp. (1533 -1584) Also known as "William the Silent". Leader of the 16th century Protestant Dutch revolt against Spain.

NEW YORK COSMOS (USA)

A story that would be echoed by LA Galaxy and David Beckham in 2007, Cosmos's colours are all about one player, Pelé.

The general manager and co-founder of the legendary American soccer team, Clive Toye, wanted the then world's most famous sportsman, Brazil's Pelé, to be the core of the team and approached him one month after the team was founded. Toye insisted on the team's colours being those of the Brazilian team to help entice Pelé. The first kit was identical to the Brazilian strip, though it changed very soon to all-green with yellow trim.

When Toye finally managed to sign his target some four years later in 1975 the kit became all-white, with the other Brazilian colours on the trim, in honour of Pelé's Brazilian club side Santos. This strategy also fulfilled another purpose: Toye stated he did not want to use the American red, white and blue in either the team's strip or badge so he could attract people from New York's immigrant population.

Cosmos folded in 1984 as the North American Soccer League (NASL) collapsed. The recently resurrected NY Cosmos, whose figurehead is former Manchester Utd legend Eric Cantona, are set to have a similar kit and badge to the original team's all-white with green and yellow trim.

NEWELL'S OLD BOYS (Argentina)

Ex-pupils of the English High School of Rosario named the team in honour of first director and football coach, Englishman Isaac Newell. The colours were chosen by the team again as a tribute to Newell; red taken from the flag of England for Newell and black for the flag of Germany, as his wife was German.

OLYMPIACOS (Greece)

The merger of the two main teams from the Greek city of Piraeus, Athlitikos Podosfairikos Pireos and Omilos Fiathlon, in 1925, gave birth to the new club Olympiacos, named in homage to the Ancient Olympic games. The colours of red for passion and white for virtue were chosen for the team; an interesting contrast to Lazio and Marseille who were inspired by the same source.

OLYMPIQUE DE MARSEILLE (France)

Like the Italian side Lazio, Olympique de Marseille's choice of colours comes from the Greek flag. The southern French club was inspired to name and clothe themselves by the revival of the Olympic movement and its ideals in the late 19th century and chose the Greek flag as a colour source in honour of the original founders of the Olympic tradition.

PALERMO (Italy)

After deciding to change from their original red and blue as it was too commonplace, the unusual colour choice of pink and black, almost unique in top-flight world football, was suggested by founding member of the club Count Giuseppe Airoldi in 1907. Airoldi said the pink and black represented the "colours of the sad and the sweet", and felt the colours a good fit for a team who experienced "results as up and down as a Swiss clock". Another club affected by Mussolini's Fascist reign in Italy, Palermo were forced to play in red and yellow, the colours of the municipality of Palermo, but switched back to the popular pink and black later.

PARMA (Italy)

One of the few Italian teams to experience as much upheaval in terms of colour choice as your average English team, Parma's original kit was yellow and blue in honour of the city's traditional colours. In an attempt to emulate the success of Juventus and inspired by their colour scheme, the team soon switched to a kit with a black cross on white shirts.

In 1990 Parma were finally promoted to Serie A after decades in the lower divisions, becoming a major force in Italian football with the financial support of Italian dairy giants Parmalat. This led to a fierce rivalry between Parma and Juve who were now often challenging for the same prizes. This rivalry led to relegation of the white and black to the away kit and Parma returned to yellow and blue hooped shirts as their first choice colour scheme.

These colours were worn through Parma's most successful period, but since the collapse of Parmalat in 2002 the white shirt with black cross has been reinstated as the home kit with the yellow and blue returning to its away kit status.

PARIS ST GERMAIN (France)

The team from the French capital get their colours from the merger of the Stade Saint-Germain club and Paris FC in 1970. The colours were combined, with the new strip being made up of Paris' red and blue and Saint-Germain's white.

PEÑAROL (Uruguay)

Uruguay's most successful team, Peñarol was formed by British railwaymen working on the new rail system in the country. Already playing cricket as part of the Central Uruguay Railway Cricket Club, they had taken for inspiration for their yellow and black strip the colours of the famous locomotive 'Rocket' designed by George Stephenson and they carried these colours over to their new football team (see p81).

PHILADELPHIA UNION (USA)

The American State of Philadelphia is proud of its heritage, being home of the great American symbol of independence the Liberty Bell. The MLS club took their colours of midnight blue and khaki from the colours worn by the revolutionary army during the war against Britain. Further cementing this patriotic link the team badge also features thirteen stars, symbolising the original thirteen colonies of America. The lighter blue piping across the chest comes from the state colour of the flag of Philadelphia and is a tribute to the supporters' group 'The Sons of Ben' named for favourite Philadephia son and Founding Father Benjamin Franklin.

REAL MADRID (Spain)

The general consensus is that Real Madrid's famous and influential all-white kit is inspired by the colours of the English amateur team Corinthians, who Arthur Johnson, also the first man to score against Barcelona for Real, supported. Johnson suggested a kit of white with a blue diagonal stripe for friendlies and the same strip with no stripe for official matches, both to be worn with a blue cloth cap. Strangely Real refer to the purple colour that appears on their kit today as trim and often as their away strip, a colour that is said to represent the region of Castille, as blue. The gold trim that is also often used is a link to their regal origins, Real meaning Royal in Spanish (see p51).

REAL SALT LAKE (USA)

The Utah club has had a close relationship with Real Madrid since their inception, hence their choice of name. The colours are said to represent certain things: red, the passion of the fans, blue for the surrounding mountains and lakes and gold for royalty. It is also probably no coincidence that these colours are also the colours of the Spanish national team.

RED BULL SALZBURG (Austria)

Originally known as SV Austria Salzburg and playing in white and purple, Salzburg, the home town team of Red Bull founder Dietrich Mateschitz, were taken over in 1997 by the energy drink billionaire and re-branded in line with his product. Salzburg now plays in Red Bull's corporate colours. This move led to a great deal of anger in Salzburg with a team being set up in a similar vein to AFC Wimbledon and FC United of Manchester in retaliation to a move that goes against the team's 60-year history.

NEW YORK RED BULLS (USA)

As well as Salzburg, Red Bull took over with far less opposition; the New York Metro Stars (now the New York Red Bulls), have formed Red Bull Brasil in São Paulo and German

team SSV Markranstädt were rebranded as RB Leipzig in Germany with a ten-year aim of reaching the Bundesliga. In the 2010-11 season all teams

played in identical home (white) and away (blue) kits and badges (but for the city name) both with a predominant Red Bull logo and but for the Brazilian team in a re-branded stadium called The Red Bull Arena.

AS ROMA (Italy)

AS Roma's colours of maroon with a gold trim represent the traditional colours of the Eternal City of Rome; the maroon is said to represent imperial dignity while the gold symbolises God in Roman Catholicism. Usually white shorts and black socks are worn; however it is traditional in games of importance that the shorts and socks are maroon as well.

ROSENBORG BK (Norway)

Rosenborg, Norway's perennial Champions League qualifiers, took their black and white colours in tribute to a local team who were successful when they were formed. As often is the case the imitators have gone on to eclipse the achievements of their inspiration, and the strange sounding black and white team they were inspired by? Odd of Skein.

ASC SAINT-ÉTIENNE (France)

The team from central France was formed in 1919 by workers of the Amicale des employés de la Société des magasins Casino (Members of the employees' Union of the Casino grocery chain). The company colours of green were chosen as the strip for the team and have

remained ever since. The strip has usually been mainly green, but striped shirts and other designs have occasionally been worn.

ST PAULI (Germany)

The most likely reason for the unique choice of brown for St Pauli, was that as the team was a latecomer to the Hamburg Football Association they were obliged to choose a colour scheme different to other teams. There was some criticism of the team's colours in Germany when the Nazi party rose to power with its association with 'the brown shirts' favoured by followers of the party, though this was not enough to force St Pauli to change colours. In recent years the fans of the club have gone completely the other way: adopting the skull and crossbones as their unofficial logo, they have a reputation for being a party club with strong anti-fascist and pro-alternative lifestyle choices, such as punk and homosexuality.

SAMPDORIA (Italy)

The Genoa team were formed by the combinations of two teams in 1946. As well as merging their names to form the new club, Andrea-Doria brought their blue colours, while the famous white, red and black mid-section came from the other club, Sampierdarenese.

SEATTLE SOUNDERS (USA)

The colours of the Washington State team are named as Sounder Blue, for the waters of the local Puget Sound; Rave Green, representing the forests of the Pacific Northwest and Cascade Shale, representing the Cascade Mountain Range. Only in America...

SPARTA PRAGUE (Czech Republic)

Club president Dr Otakar Petrik saw Arsenal play while visiting England in 1906. He decided that the colour, then dark red before Arsenal's famous white sleeve combination had been introduced, should replace the club's original black with a large 'S' emblazoned on it and took a set back to Prague (see p40). Sparta have gone on to be the most successful Czech team in history.

SPORTING LISBON (Portugal)

Sporting Lisbon have, over the years, played in various combinations of green and white including halved shirts with (usually) black shorts. The green was said by one of the club's founders the Viscount of Alvalade to symbolise hope. The hooped

style kit that they often wear is known as the "Stromp Kit" in homage to Francisco Stromp, one of Lisbon's all-time greats.

THE STRONGEST (Bolivia)

The board of the fantastically named The Strongest were unsure of a colour scheme until a friend of the founders sent them a shirt of dark green and yellow. Struck that the colours were similar to a local bird, the Chayñita, the team decided to adopt the similar yellow and black striped shirt, which they have worn since 1908.

TOULOUSE (France)

The French club was re-born in 1970 after the previous Toulouse folded after it merged with Red Star Paris. The violet colour of Toulouse's kit is a reference to the city's nickname *la Cité des violettes*, which translates as the *City of Violets*.

The city has another nickname, *Ville Rose (the Pink City)*, a colour sometimes worn by the club as an away kit.

UNIVERSITARIO DE DEPORTES (Peru)

Known as Universitario or just plain 'U', Peru's most successful team gained their colours from another laundry accident: this time the laundry was rushed by the club management into washing the strip before a big game. The laundry didn't take the team's red badges off the white shirts before washing them; this led to a cream coloured

set of shirts. Winning the game, the colours were adopted as a good luck charm.

CR VASCO DA GAMA (Brazil)

Vasco da Gama's earliest kit was black with a white tie and a belt. In 1929, the tie and belt were removed, with the kit becoming all black. In the 1930s, the white diagonal sash was added. It was introduced by Ondino Viera, the club manager at the time, the sash being part of the design of his previous team, River Plate.

VILLARREAL (Spain)

In 1947 the son of the club's president was dispatched to Valencia to purchase replacement shirts for their white and black shorts kit where, finding there were no white strips, he panicked and bought yellow. Luckily the players liked them, but not the combination of yellow and black, so he then bought some white shorts and dyed them blue at the player's behest. This combination, as well as the club's ability to best the 'big ships' of Barcelona and Real Madrid (and less positively go up and down the divisions), led to the club getting the nickname the 'Yellow Submarine' after the Beatles' 1966 hit.

VFL WOLFSBURG (Germany)

In 1945 the new team of VFL Wolfsburg was formed only seven years after the city itself had been founded to house the workers of the new Volkswagen factory. With many shortages in the post-war Germany of 1945, trainer Bernd Elberskirch managed to cobble together ten green jerseys for the team; meanwhile the town's public donated white bed sheets that were sewn together to make the team's shorts. In a reversal of the trend of a team taking their area or town's colours, the relatively new town of Wolfsburg later adopted the green and white of the team as its own, though perhaps coincidently green is also the traditional colour of Lower Saxony, Wolfsburg's region.

WHAT A SAVE! HE CERTAINLY DESERVES THAT YELLOW INTERNATIONAL KEEPER'S SHIRT!

YES, IT'S VERY DIFFERENT FROM THE GREEN HE'D HAVE TO WEAR FOR HIS CLUB...
IN 1921, YELLOW BECAME THE STANDARD GOALKEEPER'S COLOUR FOR INTERNATIONALS, THOUGH THIS DIDN'T LAST FOR LONG...

International Teams

Political Colours

Having your team play in colours associated with its location is nothing new. As we've seen many club sides play in their local area's colours, so it would seem natural that most national teams would take on the colours of their nation's flag or emblems. Indeed this is usually the case. At the 2010 South Africa World Cup, 24 of the 32 teams wore colours directly taken from their national colours. So what traditions would lead a national team to play in another colour?

Politics of course could play a part as sport and politics often cross over in the national arena. The USA and Soviet bloc both famously boycotted Olympic Games tit-for-tat during the Cold War, South Africa were rightly ostracised during the years of apartheid and there is even talk of Iran boycotting the 2012 London Olympics due to a logo offensive to Islam.

Football is not immune from this as David Goldblatt details in his book *The Ball is Round*. On a number of occasions some countries have changed their colours albeit temporarily due to political reasons. During the politically turbulent years around the Second World War this led to some unique colours: under the fascist General Franco, Spain played in blue (the colour of Franco's party) rather than the traditional red. Mussolini's fascist Italy turned out for the quarter-finals of the 1938 World Cup against their virulent

anti-fascist neighbours France in an away kit not of their traditional white, but an ominous all-black, the colour of Mussolini's fascist 'Black shirts'. During this dark time for Europe, Austria was absorbed into Nazi Germany; in the last game before this process was complete Austria recalled their retired star Matthias Sindelar. Sindelar insisted his team play in the Austrian imperial colours of red and white and he inspired them to a victory against the Nazi authorities' wishes that a draw was the preferred result.

Politics and football still mix today, and there was some criticism of Germany's 2010 World Cup black away kit, with its World War Two connotations, although this combination was in fact based on the colours worn by a German XI that had played an unofficial international in Paris in the late 19th century. While Slovenia's kit led to heated controversy and debate in only their second World Cup (see p104).

Less sinister, the 2010 South Africa World Cup, the first on the continent, saw the four Puma-sponsored teams wearing the Africa Unity strip as their third choice (left). The strip, a light blue fading half way down the shirt into a brown that continued through shorts and socks with gold trim, was designed to represent Africa's sun, skies and rich soil. The earthy brown of the jersey was, according to Puma, created by mixing actual soil samples from Cameroon, Ghana, Ivory Coast, and South Africa.

AUSTRALIA

Australia's fierce rivalry with Great Britain has led to many of sport's greatest moments, though usually involving a trophy about two inches high. Likewise their national football team gets their colours from the nation's increased independence from Great Britain. The 'Socceroos' as well as many of Australia's sporting teams including their cricket and swimming team, are outfitted in various combinations of yellow and green inspired from the colours of the flower the Golden Wattle, their national floral emblem, which is also used as a symbol for the Order of Australia, similar to the British honours system.

BRAZIL

Although the Brazilian national team's famous colours clearly are associated with their national flag, this was not always the case. Up until the 1950 World Cup (hosted by Brazil) the team played in all white. Following defeat in what was effectively the final against Uruguay, the nation went, from all accounts, into a kind of mourning. Alex Bellos in his book *Futebol: The Brazilian Way of Life* details how various Brazilian writers have described it as 'Our Hiroshima' or 'Our Waterloo'. As well as a public furore that led to the virtual demonisation of the goalkeeper Barbosa, the colours were deemed to be not patriotic enough. The newspaper *Correio da Manhã* held a competition to design a new kit, which would incorporate the four colours of the Brazilian flag. Nineteen-year-old Aldyr Garcia Schlee drew the winning design. The combination that has perhaps become the most famous international team strip of all was first used in 1954 against Chile. Hoping perhaps to emulate the dazzling play of Socrates and Falcão the famous kit has been used as an away kit by club sides worldwide including Barnsley, Crystal Palace, Newcastle United, Cowdenbeath and Bayern Munich.

Brazil's own away kit (blue shirts, white shorts and socks) evolved directly from the home kit. In the 1958 World Cup final, Brazil's opponents were the hosts Sweden, who also wear yellow. A draw to see who would wear yellow was won by the hosts and Brazil, who had travelled with no alternative kit, purchased a set of blue shirts and sewed on the badges cut from their yellow shirts. After winning the game 5-2 the colours were adopted permanently.

ENGLAND

For the first international game (against Scotland, played in November 1872 at the West Scotland Cricket ground) England wore white shirts with the famous Three Lions badge that remain fundamentally the same to this day. Though at first

glance it may seem that the English colours had been, like other later international teams, taken from the national flag, it is probably a combination of a number of factors.

White in the Victorian period was often seen as the colour of the gentleman. In cricket and tennis, both sports developed in their modern forms in England and in athletics white was the colour of the kit. At this time the only class in Britain with the time for sporting activities was the class of the gentlemen. The only place to play these games was at the private schools such as Oxbridge, Harrow and Eton. The colour was seen as dissociating the wearer from manual labour or a dirty environment, while in highly formal social functions, the traditional dress for men attending is referred to as white tie. The early England players, Corinthian and amateur in their attitude wore white as their birthright.

Another factor in the choice of the England football team's famous white shirts could well be the links between early football in England and the already established game of cricket. Cricketers of course play in white. Charlie Alcock was the secretary of Surrey County Cricket Club from 1872 to 1907 and was a prolific sportsman and sports organiser; in terms of cricket, he as a member of the MCC, was responsible for organising the first cricket Test match played in England at the Oval between England and Australia in 1880. In terms of football, he was one of the primary driving forces behind its early development.

Charles Alcock was undeniably one of football's most important figures in its history. Not only was he at the meeting where the FA brought in the height of the crossbar (then tape) and the offside rule, but he was also the founder of Wanderers, who won the first FA Cup played at the Oval (also the most famous early cricketer of them all, WG Grace, played football for Wanderers, though Grace wasn't in that FA Cup winning team). Alcock was also secretary of the FA and the proposer of the FA Cup, and was also the instigator for that first football international in 1872. With such a prestigious organiser it would not be impossible to surmise that he had something to do with the colours chosen for England. Further evidence of this cricket link can be seen by looking at the first badge adorning that shirt. The Three Lions crest has been associated with England since Richard the Lionheart in 1198 and for the first international, England walked out with a Three Lions badge with a crown above it, very similar to the England cricket badge. In fact it wasn't until 1949 that it was re-designed, by the Royal College of Arms, primarily to differentiate it to the cricket badge, the crown disappearing and the ten Tudor Roses added to symbolise the ten FA regions of England.

Comparing again with most nations' adoption of the colours of the flag as their colours, with England adopting white shirts, for whatever reason, it is still the dominant colour of the English flag the cross of St. George, so why did the team's shorts end up blue and not red, the colour of the cross? Again the links with the amateur gentlemen must be considered. For these early games many players provided their own jerseys and shorts. The shorts, it seems, were at first white, but were soon established as blue. There is evidence that often shorts would be of different colours in the same game as players simply wore their club shorts. The influence of that other famous early amateur team, the Corinthians, cannot be discounted in relation to the blue shorts. Formed in 1881 by Nicholas 'Pa' Jackson, their aim was to challenge the supremacy of a Scotland team dominated by the Queen's Park club side, who played together on a regular basis. Jackson brought the best English amateur players together to play essentially 'touring' games outside their club commitments. The success of this venture, at least in bringing the players together, is pointed out by Richard Sanders in his book *Beastly Fury*... "for most of the 1880s Jackson's promise that playing for the Corinthians was a sure step up to an international cap often proved true. In 1886, when Blackburn Rovers' J.H. Forrest became the first acknowledged professional to play for England (and was forced to wear that different-coloured shirt, a slight

The England Badge: On the left the modern day cricket badge of the England team, on the right the first football team badge.

on his non-amateur status), nine of his team-mates were Corinthians. By 1892 forty-four Corinthians had played for England." For two England matches against Wales in 1894 and 1895, the entire team consisted of members of the club. The colours of the Corinthians? White shirts, originally simply cricket shirts and blue shorts.

Though England's away kit has been many colours including sky-blue and even the awful grey of Euro 96, red is undoubtably the most famous. England had originally played in blue away shirts, however after the infamous 1-0 defeat to the part-timers of the USA in the 1950 World Cup which dumped them out of their first World Cup in the first round, England immediately dropped the blue and the next time colours clashed, the team wore the now famous red instead.

Somewhat bucking tradition, England's home kit for the 2012 European Championships is the first in 140 years to completely do away with the traditional blue, sporting a white kit with red trim and crest, colours that echo the St. George's cross.

FRANCE (Away)

Although the French away kit has always been white, one of the three colours of the French Tricolour, the 2011 strip takes its inspiration from another source. The Marinière, a white shirt with thin blue hoops, first appeared in the 19th century as the uniform of the French navy. It was later seen as civilian wear in the early 20th century, and became a symbol and icon of French culture.

Whether the Marinière style becomes the regular away kit or is just a product of a slick manufacturer's marketing strategy remains to be seen.

GERMANY

Germany and during the Cold War years West Germany have always played in a strip of white shirts and black shorts, despite their flag being made up of black, red and gold bands (apart from during the Nazi years). The white and black in fact come from the old Germanic state of Prussia whose flag is white with black borders on the top and bottom

and an eagle crest.

The German away kit is traditionally green and white; there is a widespread urban myth that this was a mark

AS THE TEAMS LINE UP AT WEMBLEY THE SUPPORTERS LOOK FORWARD TO THE GAME...
WOW! WHY ARE NEITHER TEAM WEARING THEIR HOME STRIP, SURELY ONLY ONE OF THEM NEEDS TO CHANGE?

IT'S BECAUSE IN ANY FA CUP TIE, BOTH TEAMS ARE OBLIGED TO CHANGE TO THEIR AWAY SHIRTS! *
* THIS RULE WAS IN PLACE UNTIL 1989.

of respect that Ireland retained neutrality in WWII, or they played their first post-war friendly against them; however neither of these stories are true (it was in fact

Switzerland who West Germany first played a post-war friendly against in 1950). The colours of the away kit actually reflect the colours found on the flag of the second biggest kingdom of ancient Germany; Hannover and Saxony.

GREECE

Although the white of Greece's kit does reflect one of the predominant colours of their flag, Greece played in blue until their

unexpected victory in Euro 2004 in only their, at the time, third ever appearance at either a World Cup or European Championship final stages. After their successful tournament they adopted the colour as their permanent first kit colour.

NORTHERN IRELAND and THE REPUBLIC OF IRELAND

The two Irelands colours have developed and twisted around each other much like their troubled history over the course of the 20th century.

Originally as one nation, the Irish played their first international (against England in 1882) in a kit consisting of blue shirts, white shorts and blue socks. The blue came from the colours of the Order of St Patrick, the senior order of chivalry in Ireland dating back to 1783, though it has also been noted that blue was used as a woad-stain colour by the ancient Celts. Against Scotland the team would change to a green-shirted kit, possibly borrowed from the amateur team.

When the two associations split in 1921 the Northern Irish team carried on wearing blue until switching to green in 1930, (though they kept blue socks for some time) while their southern

counterparts immediately switched to the more familiar colour. Green has been associated with Ireland since St Patrick reputedly used the shamrock to explain the Holy Trinity. During the early days after the split there are several instances of players turning out for both associations.

Blue has made a reappearance since the more commercially aware 1990s in the Northern Irish kit, with a red and white away kit to reflect the colours of Ulster. The Republic too has brought back blue, mainly as a trim, but has incorporated the orange of the Irish tricolour more often since the early 1980s.

ITALY

The Italian national team wears blue as this was the traditional colour of the House of Savoy, the ruling royal house of Italy until World War Two. This has led to the nickname for the team of the 'Azzuri' – 'the Blues'.

Blue, however, was not always the first choice. Italy began playing international football in 1910. At this time the dominant club side in Italian football was provincial side Pro Vercelli and their colour, white, was worn as Italy's first kit in homage to them. Vercelli, who won the

championship from 1908 to 1913 (only losing in 1909-10 after fielding a youth team against Inter in a protest over scheduling) provided nine of the team against Belgium in 1913 and though the national team switched to blue from their third match, the white of Pro Vercelli has been used as their away kit to this day.

JAPAN

The Japanese national team play in their blue-shirted kit as this colour represents fair play in Japan. The Japanese Football Association have encouraged the nickname 'Samurai Blues' since the 2006 World Cup.

NETHERLANDS

Royal links give the Dutch their famous colours; the orange home jersey coming from the traditional colour of their most famous regent William I of Orange (see p81), while the away kit is often 'Nassau Blue' after the current royal family.

NEW ZEALAND

The New Zealand football team had originally wanted to carry on the country's sporting tradition of wearing an all-black kit. As FIFA at the time only allowed the referee to wear black they instead chose the opposite colour of white. Their nickname is a play on the famous 'All-Blacks' nickname of their rugby

union team, the football team being known as the 'All-Whites'.

SCOTLAND

Scotland's first club side Queen's Park took a pivotal role in the first ever international against England in 1872, the team providing all eleven players and wearing their club strip of dark blue jerseys, white shorts and red socks. The colours were adopted as the national colours and worn, with a few shorts and sock changes, ever since. The influential Queen's Park club, however, changed to black and white hoops in 1873 (see p61).

Scotland have used many different colours for their away kits over the years, mainly white with navy blue trim, a natural reversal of the home kit. They have also often used yellow, a colour seen on the badge of the

Scottish FA and also on the Arms of Scotland. Pink has also been used, probably harking back to an early Scots home kit of pink and yellow hoops which were the racing colours of Archibald Primrose, the 5th Earl of Rosebery, who was an early backer of football in Scotland. Not immune to the commercial aberrations of the 90s, one or two of Scotland's away kits from this period are probably best forgotten!

SLOVENIA

After becoming again a nation in its own right in 1991 Slovenia played in the colours of the national flag, white, blue and red. In 1994 the Slovenian FA changed the colours to the white and green colours of Ljubljana, the capital city, and also of the most successful club at the time, Ljubljana's NK Olimpija.

This unpopular move led to much dissent in the wider country with campaigns for the traditional colours.

Though the debate raged on,

the 2010 World Cup saw the new colours still in use with Slovenia playing in white with green diagonal lines representing the Triglav Mountains, the nation's highest peak (a design that features on the crest of their flag). The away strip was green with lime lines, representing the lime tree, which is another national symbol.

The campaigners however have won the day and from 2012, the colours will change back to the traditional colours with a white first choice strip and blue for away matches.

TEAM GB

At the 1908 London Olympics club side Upton Park (no link to West Ham) represented and won gold for Great Britain wearing essentially the England kit with a Union Jack crest, reflecting the English FA's control of the team. This was worn for all Olympics GB qualified for, the last being 1960. Outside the Olympics a British XI ran out in the 1947 'Match of the Century' playing a European XI to celebrate the Home Nations re-joining FIFA, wearing navy blue as the match was played in Scotland.

In 1955 another British XI played a Europe XI, this time at Belfast's Windsor Park to celebrate the Northern Irish FA's 75th anniversary, again wearing the host nation's colour, this time green.

The men's and women's teams for the 2012 Olympics have been embroiled in controversy from the start, with the Northern Irish, Scottish and Welsh FAs opposing a British team. The strip too has been criticised, with Stella McCartney's re-jigged Union Jack design labelled as being blue.

WALES

Of course red is the predominant national colour of Wales, the famous red dragon appearing on the country's flag. The most likely origin of the red shirts and white shorts that the Welsh team wear was in emulation of the colours of the rugby union side; previously the football team had worn a jersey of green and white halves, the colours which are on the nation's flag behind the dragon. The most common change colours of Wales have been various combinations of yellow and green, which can be seen on the shield on the Welsh FA's crest.

The winning colour

Man. Utd (19)
Liverpool (18)
Arsenal (13)
Nott. Forest (1)

Everton (8)
Chelsea (4)
Man. City (3)
Portsmouth (2)
Ipswich (1)

Aston Villa (7)
Burnley (2)

Leeds (3)
Derby County (2)
Preston N.E. (2)
Tottenham (2)

Sheff. Wed* (4)
Huddersfield (3)
West Brom (1)

Football League Champions

1889-2012 Summary – 113 Championships

So does it matter? Alex Ferguson definitely would think so. As well as dominating English football with his Red Devils of Manchester Utd for the last twenty-five or so years, his time at the similarly coloured Aberdeen led to the breaking of the dominance of the Glasgow clubs of Celtic and Rangers, with three Scottish league wins, plus numerous domestic and European trophies. For Fergie, red is the colour.

Red is often cited as a powerful colour, a lucky colour around the world. In England it has become part of the footballing history of the country, with Liverpool's dominance during the 70s and 80s, not to mention years of continued success by Arsenal and the aforementioned dominance of the Premier League era by Ferguson's United. It was perhaps cemented in English culture by England's one moment of glory in the 1966 World Cup, when Bobby Moore and co. ran out in the red away kit to defeat West Germany. A University of Chichester report even claimed that goalkeepers should wear red, as the opposition will be more likely to miss penalties against them!

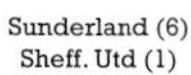
Sunderland (6)
Sheff. Utd (1)

Newcastle Utd

Blackburn Rovers

Wolves

Everton**

Of course the other side to this argument is strong too. Teams have had their moment in the sun not playing in red, the golden Wolves team of the 50s or Leeds in white in the mid-70s for example. In Scotland, despite Aberdeen's brief success in the 80s, the green hoops of Celtic and blue of Rangers share 97 championships at the time of writing between them, while in Italy the black and white of Juventus dominate and Real Madrid, resplendent in white still lead the list of European Cup titles, winning nine times.

A look at the English league winners makes interesting reading, especially the staggering statistic that there were nineteen winners wearing stripes before the Second World War and none since!

Maybe it's time for another shift in the colour fortunes of English football? Perhaps all it needs is someone to come along with deep pockets and purchase a team that wears blue...?

* First three championships as The Wednesday.

** Everton's kit for their 1890-91 season.

Note on Sources

While researching this book I have read a number of fantastic books and used some excellent websites to gather the information. If you are interested in learning any more about the origins of the game I would highly recommend Richard Sander's *Beastly Fury: The Strange Birth of British Football* published by Bantam Books. For books on the game around the world Phil Ball's *Morbo: the Story of Spanish Football*, Ulrich Hess-Lichenberger's *Tor! The Story of German Football* both published by WSC, John Foot's *Calcio: A History of Italian Football* published by Harper and *Futebol: The Brazilian Way of Life* by Alex Bellos and published by Bloomsbury books are all excellent reads.

Thanks for their correspondences go to: Lawrence Bland, Club Archivist for Morecambe FC, Gary Bray of Rotherham FC, John Brockwell of MK Dons Supporters' Association, Mick Collins, author of *Roy of the Rovers: The Unauthorised Biography*, Jason Gilham of the Colorado Rapids, Paul Goddfrey, Director of Cheltenham Town FC, Mike Harrison of the Wyggeston School, Colin Hendrie of the Independent Manchester United Supporters' Association, John Lerwill, Official Historian for Aston Villa FC, Jeremy McIlwaine, Conservative Party Archivist and Peter Wynne-Thomas, Archivist of Nottinghamshire County Cricket Club.

I chose, when writing this book, to concentrate on the reasons behind a team's choice of colours. Not only is this format not suitable to document the myriad of minor changes that team's kits go under every year, but also it was what really interested me. If you are interested in looking into the ever-changing evolution of British teams' kits I would suggest the excellent website www.historicalkits.co.uk which provides more detail on subtle changes over the years and up to date information on the subject than a book ever could.

List of Players

The style of kit was chosen to best represent each team, each player was chosen to represent their club or country with the hope they are held in affection by supporters. The era of kit and player may not necessarily match.

Aberdeen - *Gordon Strachan*
Accrington Stanley - *Paul Mullin*
AC Milan - *Ruud Gullit*
AEK Athens - *Mimis Papaioannou*
African Unity - *Didier Drogba*
Ajax - *Johan Neeskens*
Aldershot Town - *Anthony Charles*
Alianza Lima - *Teófilo Cübillas*
RSC Anderlecht - *Paul Van Himst*
Arbroath - *Walter Cameron*
Arsenal (old) - *Joe Shaw*
Arsenal (new) - *Liam Brady*
Aston Villa - *Paul McGrath*
Athletic Bilbao - *Pichichi*
Ath. Independiente - *Ricardo Bochini*
Atlético Madrid - Luis Aragonés
Australia - *Lucas Neill*
Ayr United - *Peter Price*

Barcelona - *Lionel Messi*
Barnet - *Les Eason*
Barnsley - *Ernie Hine*
Bayern Munich - *Franz Beckenbauer*
Belgrano de Córdoba - *Lucas Parodi*
Birmingham City - *Trevor Francis*
Blackburn Rovers - *Alan Shearer*
Blackpool - *Stanley Matthews*
Boca Juniors - *Diego Maradona*
Bolton Wanderers - *Nat Lofthouse*
Borussia Dortmund - *Matthias Sammer*
Botafogo - *Garrincha*
AFC Bournemouth - *Dickie Dowsett*
Bradford City - *Dean Windass*
SC Braga - *Albert Meyong*
Brazil - *Zico*
Brentford - *Ken Coote*
Brighton & Hove A. - *Mark Lawrenson*
Bristol City - *John Ateyo*
Bristol Rovers - *Jack Pitt*
Burnley - *Leighton James*
Burton Albion - *John McGrath*
Bury - *Norman Bullock*

Cambridge Utd - *Lindsey Smith*
Cardiff City - *Fred Keenor*
Carlisle United - *Chris Balderstone*
Celtic - *Danny McGrain*
Charlton Athletic - *Keith Peacock*
Chelsea - *Kerry Dixon*
Chester City - *Lee Dixon*
Chesterfield - *Ernie Moss*
Chicago Fire - *Brian McBride*
Colchester Utd - *Micky Cook*
Colorado Rapids- *Pablo Mastroeni*
Corinthians (Eng) - *C. B. Fry*
Corinthians (Bra) - *Socrates*
Coventry City - *Dion Dublin*
Crawley Town - *Pablo Mills*
Crewe Alexandra - *Frank Lord*
Crystal Palace - *Ian Wright*

Dagenham & Redbridge - *Jon Nurse*
Derby County - *Dave MacKay*
Dundee - *Doug Cowie*
Dundee United - *Maurice Malpas*
Dunfermline Athletic - *Norris McCathie*
Dynamo Moscow - *Vladimir Torshentsev*

List of Players
Continued

England (home) - *Bobby Moore*
England (away) - *Geoff Hurst*
England (cricket) - *W.G. Grace*
Enosis Neon Paralimni - *Dimitris Kizas*
RCD Espanyol - *Daniel Jarque*
Everton - *Dixie Dean*
Exeter City - *Tony Kellow*

Falkirk - *Russell Latapy*
Fenerbahce - *Ümit Özat*
AFC Fiorentina - *Giancarlo Antognoni*
First Vienna - *Hans Buzek*
Fleetwood Town - *Nathan Pond*
France - *Florent Malouda*
Fulham - *Johnny Haynes*

Galatasaray - *Hakan Sükür*
Germany (home) - *Paul Breitner*
Germany (away) - *Jürgen Klinsmann*
Gillingham - *Andy Hessenthaler*
IFK Gothenburg - *Roland Nilsson*
Grasshopper Zurich - *Alfred Bickel*
Greece - *Theodoras Zayorakis*
Greenock Morton - *Allan McGraw*

Hamilton Academical - *Richard Offiong*
Hartlepool United - *Keith Houchen*
Heart of Midlothian - *John Cummings*
Hereford United - *Mel Pejic*
Hibernian - *Eddie Turnbull*
Hull City - *Chris Chilton*

Independiente - *Ricardo Bochini*
Inter Milan - *Giacinto Facchetti*
Inverness Cal. Th. - *Adam Rooney*
Ipswich Town - *John Wark*
Italy - *Paolo Maldini*

Japan - *Daisuke Matsu*
Juventus - *Alessandro Del Pierro*

Kilmarnock - *Andy Kerr*
FC Koln - *Wolfgang Overath*

Lazio - *Paolo Di Canio*
Leicester City - *Gary Lineker*
Leeds United - *Billy Bremner*
RC Lens - *Marc-Vivien Foé*
Leyton Orient - *John Chiedozie*
Lincoln City - *Grant Brown*
Liverpool - *Kenny Daglish*
Livingston - *Marvin Andrews*
LA Galaxy - *David Beckham*
Luton town - *Mark Stein*

Macclesfield Town - *Darren Tinson*
Manchester City - *Francis Lee*
Manchester United - *Bobby Charlton*
Melchester Rovers - *Roy Race*
Middlesbrough - *Juninho*
Millwall - *Tony Cascarino*
MK Dons - *Dean Lewington*
AS Monaco - *Glenn Hoddle*
Morecambe - *Jim Bentley*
Motherwell - *Ian St John*

Netherlands - *Johan Cruyff*
Newcastle - *Peter Beardsley*
Newell's Old Boys - *Gabriel Heinze*
New York Cosmos - *Pelé*
New York Red Bulls - *Thierry Henry*
New Zealand - *Wynton Rufer*
Northampton Town - *John Frain*
Northern Ireland - *George Best*
Norwich City - *Justin Fashanu*
Nottingham Forest - *John Robertson*
Notts County - *Albert Iremonger*

Oldham Athletic - *Andy Ritchie*
Olympiacos - *Yves Triantafillos*
Olympique Marseille - *Chris Waddle*
Oxford United - *Steve Foster*

Palermo - *Roberto Biffi*
Paris St. Germain - *George Weah*
Parma - *Hernan Crespo*
Partick Thistle - *Jackie Campbell*
Peñarol - *Severino Varela*
Peterborough United - *Tommy Robson*
Philadelphia Union - *Eduardo Coudet*
Plymouth Argyle - *Paul Mariner*
Portsmouth - *Jimmy Dickinson*
Port Vale - *Roy Sproson*
Preston North End - *Tom Finney*

Queen's Park - *Andrew Watson*
Queens Park Rangers - *Trevor Sinclair*

Raith Rovers - *Andy Young*
Rangers - *Ally McCoist*
Reading - *Leroy Lita*
Real Madrid - *Ferenc Puskas*
Real Salt Lake - *Freddy Adu*
Red Bull Salzburg - *Christian Schwegler*
Referee - *Pierluigi Collina*
Rep. of Ireland - *Robbie Keane*
Rochdale - *Gary Jones*
AS Roma - *Aldair*
Rosenborg BK - *Roar Strand*
Ross County - *Don Cowie*
Rotherham United - *Shaun Goater*

Saint-Étienne - *Michel Platini*
St Mirren - *Frank McAvennie*
St Johnstone - *John Brogan*
St Pauli - *Jürgen Gronau*
Sampdoria - *Roberto Mancini*
Scotland - *Graeme Souness*
Scunthorpe United - *Jack Brownsword*
Seattle Sounders - *Brad Evans*
Sheffield United - *Harry Johnson*
Sheffield Wednesday - *Alan Finney*
Shrewsbury Town - *Mickey Brown*
Slovenia - *Zlatko Zahovic*
Southampton - *Matt Le Tissier*
Southend United - *Kevin Maher*
Sparta Prague - *Tomas Repka*
Sporting Lisbon - *Mario Jardel*
Stevenage Borough - *Jon Aston*
Stockport County - *Jack Connor*
Stoke City - *Eric Skeels*
Sunderland - *Barry Venison*
Swansea City - *Ivor Allchurch*
Swindon Town - *Don Rogers*

Team GB - *Jack Rodwell*
The Strongest - *Óscar Carmelo Sanchez*
Torquay - *Kevin Hill*
Tottenham Hotspur - *Jimmy Greaves*
Toulouse - *Yannik Stopyra*
Tranmere Rovers - *John Aldridge*

Universitario - *Teodaro Fernandez*

Vasco Da Gama - *Roberto Dinamite*
Villarreal - *Juan Román Riquelme*

Wales - *John Hartson*
Walsall - *David Kelly*
Watford - *John Barnes*
West Bromwich Albion - *Cyrille Regis*
West Ham United - *Trevor Brooking*
Wigan Athletic - *Peter Atherton*
AFC Wimbledon - *John Fashanu*
Wolverhampton Wanderers - *Steve Bull*
Wrexham - *Mickey Thomas*
Wycombe Wanderers - *Chris Vinnicombe*

Yeovil Town - *Ike Clarke*
York City - *Andy McMillan*

Those that got away

Ayr United

Burton Albion

Carlisle United

Crawley Town

Crewe Alexandra

Greenock Morton

Hamilton Academicals

Hartlepool United

Stevenage Borough

Apologies to British supporters if your team is not in this book, but every effort was undertaken, including contacting your club. If you have any information that may help, please feel free to contact me through Pitch Publishing and I will do my best to add any information in any future editions of *Picking up the Threads*.